Trans[...]
Your Library
into a Learning
Playground

Transforming Your Library into a Learning Playground

A Practical Guide for Public Librarians

Brittany R. Jacobs

LIBRARIES UNLIMITED
An Imprint of ABC-CLIO, LLC
Santa Barbara, California • Denver, Colorado

Copyright © 2018 by Brittany R. Jacobs

All rights reserved. No part of this publication may be reproduced, stored in a retrieval system, or transmitted, in any form or by any means, electronic, mechanical, photocopying, recording, or otherwise, except for the inclusion of brief quotations in a review, without prior permission in writing from the publisher.

Library of Congress Cataloging in Publication Control Number: 2017036907

ISBN: 978–1–4408–5730–0 (paperback)
      978–1–4408–5731–7 (ebook)

22 21 20 19 18   1 2 3 4 5

This book is also available as an eBook.

Libraries Unlimited
An Imprint of ABC-CLIO, LLC

ABC-CLIO, LLC
130 Cremona Drive, P.O. Box 1911
Santa Barbara, California 93116-1911
www.abc-clio.com

This book is printed on acid-free paper ∞

Manufactured in the United States of America

Contents

Preface vii

Introduction ix

CHAPTER 1: Why Play? 1

CHAPTER 2: A Perfect Location for Learning 13

CHAPTER 3: Getting to Know Your Audience 25

CHAPTER 4: Story Programming 37

CHAPTER 5: Planning Your Program 51

CHAPTER 6: Full STEAM Ahead! 65

CHAPTER 7: Grabbing and Holding Participants' Attention 79

CHAPTER 8: How to Get Repeat Visitors 91

Appendix 101

Index 111

Preface

This book is a result of years' worth of creating programs and curriculums for informal education settings, culminating with and focusing on an integrated STEM (science, technology, engineering, and math) and literacy-based spy club I created and implemented for the Free Library of Philadelphia. I'm not a teacher by trade, but that doesn't stop me from teaching at every chance that I get. As an advocate for lifelong learning habits, I have taken it upon myself to encourage children and youth to engage with information and knowledge outside of the walls of the classroom. From hosting programs in parks, museums, camps, and zoos, I have found that the library setting is ripe with potential, as it has resources and information experts in-house.

After word got around about my spy club, I began receiving e-mails from librarians all over the country, inquiring about how to create a similar program at their library. I tried to convey as much as I could within the confines of e-mails, but there is so much that goes into creating a program that, short of e-mailing them a novel, for practicality's sake I couldn't get the whole message across. What I needed to do was sit down and write out my process from conception to implementation, and so sit down and write I did! This book is not meant to enable you to copy my program; rather it is meant to inspire and equip you to create your own. Each library user population has different needs, wants, and interests, and over the next eight chapters, you will learn how to recognize those needs, wants, and interests and create your own tailor-made programs for your children and youth patrons.

With the standards of education rising every year and the onset of new technology emerging at breakneck speeds, informal education settings such as libraries have found themselves struggling to keep up to date or risk becoming irrelevant. Information that was once only found in books is now available at the touch of a finger. Computer labs, personal laptops, and smartphones have made information available to the masses. So the question must be asked: How can libraries transform themselves into relevant, exciting, and stimulating learning centers that appeal to children and youth?

This book aims to answer that question by providing readers with a step-by-step guide to creating programs by focusing on one simple concept: play. The driving force behind the theory of play or game-based learning is to engage and envelop children and youth to such an extent that learning becomes a natural and exciting process. The beauty of informal settings is that while they certainly reinforce learning standards, they are not held to them, which essentially busts open the box that many are trapped inside of.

Public libraries have an exciting opportunity to help fill the learning gap with unique ways to help children and youth learn through exploration and play. By teaching to incorporate existing programs such as maker spaces, story time, and book clubs, this book will show readers how to play to their strengths, utilize tools and resources that they already have, and transform their libraries into learning playgrounds.

Introduction

Figure I.1 Free Library of Philadelphia Espionage Agency

It was a warm day in the outskirts of Philadelphia at the Free Library's Andorra branch. I was the after-school leader (ASL), and, seeing as it was my first week on the job, I was getting to know the handful of students who used the library on a daily basis. I was sitting in a child-sized chair that accompanied a child-sized table that sat atop a child-stained carpet when a six-year-old girl came in and sat next to me; we'll call her S. She was painfully shy and wouldn't make eye contact with me or speak in anything other than short one- or two-word answers. Having overheard a group of kids the previous day talking about how cool it would to be a spy, I began to draw a simple cell phone on a piece of lined paper.

"What if I told you I was a spy?" I asked her as I cut the cell phone out.

She scrutinized me, but said nothing. The other kids went on shrieking and gabbing with one another about how so-and-so did this and that.

"Yep," I continued, and then I pretended to hear the cell phone ring. Holding it up to my ear, and excusing myself from the conversation with S, I turned, ever so slightly, away from her and began to speak with the mystery caller.

"Oh, yes. Yes. Mm-hmm. That sounds serious, but I'm sure we can handle it. Well, I have one sitting right here . . . let me check."

I held the phone out to S and told her it was for her. She looked at me like I was out of my mind, and then proceeded to look around the library to see if anyone else was witnessing what she very well may have thought was a mental breakdown.

"Sorry," I said into the phone, "she doesn't want to talk."

Still eyeing me, but refusing to interact, she leaned in a little closer as I turned in my seat to continue the "conversation."

"Okay," I sighed. "I'm really sorry she didn't want to be a part of this . . ."

I felt a tap on my shoulder, and turned to see her holding out her hand.

"I'll take it," she said looking me straight in the eyes.

"Hello?" she asked.

I began to doodle on the scraps lying on the table, as if nothing in the world was strange about having a conversation with someone via a paper cell phone. I looked up and gave her a nod of encouragement. It was silent for a few seconds, but then I heard it, and it was like music to my ears.

"You've got to be kidding me!" she said into the phone, just as another six-year-old approached the table.

"Who are you talking to?" he asked, looking at S like *she* was the crazy one. She held up her hand, just like she must have seen adults do a hundred times before, "Shh! I'm on the phone!" Turning, ever so slightly, away from the table she went back to the conversation, completely engrossed and off in her own world. After the phone call was finished, she asked if I could help make her a pair of spy glasses, to go along with the phone. Using the same lined paper, I drew and cut out glasses that she then taped to her head and wore home along with the cell phone stuck in her back pocket.

The next day S came bursting through the doors and walked briskly toward me with a look of incredible determination on her face. She was wearing the glasses made out of paper and had the cell phone tucked into the waistline of her pants. She stopped no less than 6 inches from my face, and with a severe tone said, "I know how to kidnap and torture a man."

Welcome to my job, where I have no idea what will be thrown at me on any given day. Suppressing my urge to laugh at what has just come out of this tiny and adorable girl, I stared right back at her through those lensless paper glasses and without missing a beat said, "Well, you'd better tell me how." She went on to describe how using just a chair, a piece of string, and a piece of tape one can restrain and drive a man mad—MAD I tell you! Thus began one of the most successful informal education programs that I have ever had the pleasure of creating and implementing.

Just two weeks prior, I was sitting in a six-hour orientation for the Literacy Enrichment After-School Program (LEAP) along with my fellow ASLs. It was a day filled with enthusiastic speakers telling us what important roles we were playing as soldiers in the war against illiteracy. Cheers rang out, people clapped and hollered, and the excitement for the new school year became palpable.

I had been assigned to the Andorra branch, which was in the vicinity of public, charter, and private schools. As the branch was on the outskirts of the city limit, its school assessment scores were higher than the city's average, though still shockingly low. It's hard to believe that literacy is still a problem in our modern and advanced world, yet over half of Philadelphia students entering fourth grade are reading (well) below standards. Zooming back into Philadelphia's Andorra neighborhood, my focus was on helping the kindergarten through 12th-grade students.

In gearing up for the 2015–2016 school year, I looked up the Pennsylvania System of School Assessment (PSSA) scores for the public school nearest to Andorra. Shocked, I discovered that only 36.5 percent of third- to eighth-grade students scored "Proficient" on the language arts/literature portion of the PSSA. A small group of 4.9 percent were "Advanced," leaving over 50 percent of students reading and writing below grade level (Required Federal Reporting Measures Commonwealth of Pennsylvania, 2014–2015).

According to a 2003 survey of Philadelphia adults, age 16 and older, the National Center for Education Statistics found that over 22 percent of them lacked basic necessary literacy skills. This didn't fully hit me until one day when a father of two young girls came in to the library and asked me to read him the teacher's note that was sent home with his daughters.

How incredibly difficult life must be for someone lacking these basic skills? How would you pay bills, fill out medical forms, or maneuver through society on a daily basis? We as a people are always reading: road signs, menus, e-mails, paperwork, and so on. Thanks to organizations like the Center for Literacy, there are teams of people working toward addressing adult illiteracy, and we at LEAP were focusing on the younger side of the spectrum.

Why pour funding, time, and talent into library programming? Studies show that there is a significant spike in crime during the hours of 3:00 p.m. to 6:00 p.m., which just so happens to be the time when a large portion of children are left to fend for themselves. Many parents/guardians work late into the evening, and when childcare isn't an affordable option, the children are left to get themselves home and to look after themselves. With 52 branches dispersed throughout the city limits, the Free Library of Philadelphia (FLP) saw an opportunity to create not only a safe space for children and teens to retreat to but also a nurturing environment where homework help and educational programming would be offered.

Each branch has an ASL, and they are there solely for literacy enrichment and homework help. We would be kidding ourselves if we assumed that all (or even most) children who came to the library were ready and willing to work on homework after spending hours in the classroom. On the contrary, they are ready to burst at the seams and the last thing they want to do is sit and work on assignments. I did my best to offer engaging educational activities, and pounced on every teachable moment, but I felt more could be done.

During our LEAP orientation Strategic Initiatives (SI), a department of the Free Library Foundation, came and presented an opportunity for program funding. Anyone with a programming idea was welcome to put together and submit a proposal for potential funding. Seeing that the kids at Andorra took so quickly to the "spy" theme, I began mulling over the idea of a STEM (science, technology, engineering and math) and literacy-based spy club: a place where the kids were the agents and were engaged in missions that utilized teamwork, ingenuity, and innovation on top of the aforementioned academic skills. It was a brief three-page proposal, and truth be told, soon after I submitted it in early fall, it drifted to the back of my mind as day-to-day programming demanded my time and energy.

Fall soon turned into winter, and I fell into a very comfortable rhythm at Andorra. I had a solid group of 10–16 kids on a daily basis, which was a huge improvement from the previous years' daily average of 2–6 kids. Word of mouth had spread that the library was the place to go after school, as I became a daily fixture in these kids' lives and vice versa.

After the holidays flew past, I was notified that my proposal was chosen by SI and was to be awarded $250 for a pilot program. I was called in to the SI office the following week to give a more in-depth overview of the spy club, and I quickly began writing the curriculum. The day of presentation arrived, and backed by a boldness and fire to pull off something truly magical for the kids, I went into the meeting and began divulging "top secret" information. The pitch was as follows:

> When the Free Library was founded back in 1891, it was charged with the safekeeping of a cryptex belonging to none other than Philadelphia's own Benjamin Franklin. Library staff played two roles: librarian and secret agent for the Free Library of Philadelphia Espionage Agency (FLPEA). The cryptex was hidden someplace deep in the FLP's central building under lock and key. Recently, there had been a breach in security, and the cryptex was stolen. Due to the nature of the crime, it looked to have been an inside job—a rogue librarian! Seeing as the librarians/secret agents at central had their hands full with trying to cover up this embarrassing heist, I was charged with recruiting a new generation of agents to help track down and recover the stolen cryptex. The Central Library, or headquarters, would be divulging information via video messages and missions on a weekly basis to the new agents at Andorra.
>
> This is not a mission for the faint of heart, for it will take hard work and commitment. Anyone wanting to take part in the FLPEA must go through a screening process and pass an initial training exercise. Applications including basic information and fingerprints as well as a (very) short essay portion were at hand, and should a young person be accepted into the fold (spoiler alert! everyone who applied was accepted!), then he or she would receive an official FLPEA badge and lanyard, a certificate congratulating him or her on his or her acceptance, and a lapel pin with the FLPEA logo to be worn as a sign of pride as well as recognition among fellow agents out in the field.

I had them hook, line, and sinker! My initial budget of $250 was doubled on the spot to $500! The SI team's excitement was palpable, which only served to increase my own excitement. I took three weeks to hammer out final details of the curriculum, all the while dropping little hints of an impending "situation" with my kids at Andorra. They knew I was a spy; I had told them this during the very first week when I made the paper phone, but they all thought I was a pretender of the most massive sort. They were right; however, they had no idea what was in store for them.

The week before my program was to start, I gathered small groups of kids together in a huddle and began my recruitment for the FLPEA. Understandably, they were wary to begin with, but once I showed them my official FLPEA badge and pin, they began to look at one another in a way that I could tell they were thinking something along the lines of, "she might *really* be a spy!" Now, I'm not an actress in the sense that I can get on stage or before a camera and regurgitate memorized lines, but when

I'm working with kids I can pull off Oscar-worthy performances if it will encourage exploration and imagination. The kids were hooked, and on the first meeting I had 10 eager applicants waiting to apply for the FLPEA. Although I have worked with these kids on a daily basis for six months, never had I seen them (ALL of them) so excited to read something and get to work filling it out. Based on their low reading scores, but more so on their complete disdain for anything academic, I had planned on slugging through the application for the entire two-hour time slot—for it would have taken that long to get through a single math or literature sheet. What happened reset the tone for the entire program, as it showed me the potential, not that the curriculum had, but that the kids had.

Each applicant, who ranged in age from 3 to 15 years old, was given an application and a pencil. I hung back for a minute and watched the group transform before my eyes. They were actively reading through the page, asking each other for help with words they couldn't read and sounding them out together. Shrieks of excitement rang out as they conquered word after word, sentence after sentence. I then took their fingerprints and looked over their application. Much to my surprise, the majority of the agents had left the SKILLS portion blank.

"I'm sorry," I said, "I cannot accept an incomplete application. You MUST fill out the SKILLS portion of this paper."

I received backlash, as the agents argued that they didn't have any skills because they were only kids. They didn't have any skills because they didn't score well in school. They didn't have skills because they were never told that they had any to begin with. My heart broke at this, but was quickly restored as I began to shed a different light on their abilities.

"Brandy, you are always sneaking food into the library when you know very well that we don't allow food in here. That sneakiness is a very valuable skill, especially for a spy." Her face lit up, as she began to reinforce her sneaky skill with stories of how she dominated at hide-and-seek, how she snuck into class one time and the teacher didn't notice, and so on. And so it went, taking the skills that usually got them into trouble and shedding them in a good light.

"Charlie, you lie a lot, but that means that you're good at coming up with stories on the spot—a word for that is IMPROVISATION. What a great skill to have!"

As I continued, the kids got the hang of it and were able to recognize their own skills, while wildly writing them down onto their application.
I received applications with skills such as blowing bubbles, walking backward, jumping, hugging, stealing, singing, and coloring.

Once awarded with their ID badges and pins, I gave them a hearty congratulations and brought them into the "Meeting Room" (basement) where a video message from headquarters was awaiting them. Senior Agent Wells explained the nature of the crime, as well as outlining the evidence gathered from the scene and introduced the eyewitness. The eyewitness was a fellow senior agent, and Senior Agent Wells had sent the interrogation (a note on vocabulary in Chapter 6) video for the new agents to review. An official FLPEA composite sketch sheet was passed out, and the agents drew illustrations of the perpetrator based on the verbal description from the eyewitness. The second mission for the day was to identify the fingerprints pulled from the crime scene. After reading through the mission outline that gave a brief summary of the seven fingerprint patterns used by our counterparts at the FBI, the agents were off on their own to properly identify the prints pulled and sent over to us at Andorra. Using a digital microscope and working together as a team, they were able to successfully identify the type of print pulled, and went on to identify their own fingerprint patterns. Older agents helped the younger ones, teaching them how to use the zoom function on the microscope, and conversations went back and forth when a print was difficult to identify.

The kids had a blast, and the best part was that they were having so much fun that they didn't even realize that they were not only learning but also successfully reading and writing. Though they swore to secrecy, the second week had 10 new agents eager to apply, bringing the total to 20. Each week brought new faces from all three school systems, and by the end of the three months, I had over 60 enrolled agents.

This program was a first of many sorts for all of the agents. Thanks to a generous retired shipping agent in the Philly area, I had a 9 × 14 feet world map covering an entire wall in our meeting room. FLPEA markers covered the cities where evidence was found, and tracked the rogue agent week after week as the agent was on the run. This was the first map that any of the agents had seen in person, and not a single one could place the first marker on Philadelphia, for they had no clue where it—or North America—was. By the final week, all agents could name and locate the continents, and a good portion learned how to read coordinates. This is just one example of how all-encompassing the curriculum was. Not only was it STEM and literacy based but it branched out into every field imaginable. Geography, history, languages, we even had a discussion about the war in Syria during a mission that took us to the World Seed Bank in Norway. In addition to the first time seeing/using a map, it was also the first time agents used test tubes, a digital microscope, tangrams; were part of a nonsports-related team; and were given responsibility on a large scale. This club belonged to *them*; it was successful because of *them*;

and they gained a sense of pride and accomplishment because the FLPEA and the FLP were counting on *them* to solve the case.

On Tuesdays (meeting days), the kids stood a little taller, their vocabulary was stronger, and they worked as a cohesive team. They were in on a TOP SECRET mission and it thrilled them to no end. Their schoolwork began to intersect with the missions, as they began to connect and apply one with the other. When working on math homework, one child recounted how the quipu used during a FLPEA mission sent from Mexico was very similar to the counting groups she was being asked to use on her homework. During an ice-melt mission that had us tracking the rogue agent in the Antarctic, one agent yelled out, "Hey! This is kind of like science!" I held my breath. *They've figured me out! Now they know they're learning and will quit!*

"Yeah," came another agent, "but this is way more fun!"

Phew!

I kept increasing the difficultly of the weekly missions, as the agents kept rising to the occasion and surpassing my expectations. Quickly I had agents using binary code, identifying gasses in nebulae, and tracking down precise coordinates on maps, just to name a few of the many challenges. These kids, who consistently underscored on tests and who on the first day of spy club believed they had no skills, were succeeding with flying colors. They had what it took and more. All they needed was a new environment where failure was a key part of success. Each failed attempt to complete a task was a chance for them to learn and revise their initial approach. No grades were handed out, so the stress of quantitative measurement was thrown out the window. The club proponent of this program turned everything into a group project, which helped to sharpen communication, problem-solving, and teamwork skills. Had I tried to pull this off in the school setting, I believe it wouldn't have worked. The library was far enough removed from their school life, yet it was still a pertinent part of their daily activities, which made for the perfect setting.

Trends toward *educational* after-school programming are becoming stronger by the minute, giving libraries a unique and ripe opportunity to usher in transformative change. Maker spaces, STE(A)M events, coding clubs, and the like are popping up at breakneck speed, with libraries being a key player in the game. Free access to programs and information, safe spaces for all, and resource experts on hand are just a few of the assets that can turn your library into an exciting and relevant learning playground.

With a background in children's programming and experience teaching in a wide variety of informal education settings, I have seen what does and what does not work when trying to engage children. I've seen organizations spend thousands of dollars that had a low success rate, while places with a shoestring budget knocked the ball out of the park. By no means do I claim to be an expert on play theory, or program development. All I can claim is to be passionate about engaging children with knowledge, and to have stumbled upon some success with programs I've developed.

This book is my attempt to help shed some light on the power of play in programs for kids of all ages, as well as the reasons behind why public libraries are a perfect setting for establishing a learning playground. The next eight chapters will provide readers with the tools and thought processes necessary to create and implement integrated, educational, and innovative programs for children and youth. Using my spy club program in Philadelphia as an exemplar, I will share stories and unpack the process of thinking, writing, planning, and executing programs that will transform your library into an exciting learning playground!

CHAPTER 1

Why Play?

Learning through Play Isn't Only for Early Childhood Development

What Is Play?

It was 100 degrees outside, with near 100 percent humidity. I had 30 antsy six-year-olds stuck in a classroom because our schedule to go and see the Komodo dragon had been bumped back by 10 minutes. Now, 10 minutes may not seem like a terribly long time, but when you've got 30 squirmy kids, one of which was threatening to cut another's hair off, all vying for your attention but with nothing planned, then 10 minutes will stretch out into 10 years. To regain control of the classroom, and to curb the scissor threats being thrown around, I got down on the floor and began to tell a story just above the level of a whisper. Immediately kids sat down next to and around me and began shushing each other so they could hear. "The cheetah was running, running, RUNNING through the tall, tall grass! He heard a strange noise, and turned around just in time to see a . . ." It was then that I pointed to a boy sitting very nicely who was rapt with attention. After a moment, he realized that I wanted him to tell us what the cheetah saw, and he said, "A giant walking pizza!" A wave of giggles washed over the entire class, as I continued on with the giant pizza chasing the cheetah. For the climax of every sentence, I pointed to another child for him or her to fill in the details of the story. This "popcorn game" quickly became a favorite to play throughout the summer.

Due to the nature of my career path (i.e., working with children in informal education settings), I'm asked to play on a weekly, if not daily, basis. I play board games, make-believe games, music, and everything in-between. Playing is a large part of how I interact with young people, and it's something that I highly value. It's through playing that I'm able to connect with children quickly and in a nonthreatening manner. As often as I do engage with play, I find it to be a curious, yet powerful, thing. It's used as an incentive for good behavior and as a channel to release excess energy (in the hope of curbing poor behavior). The way we play changes as we get older, as does the frequency.

It's obvious that most kids engage in play in some form or another; but how important can playing really be? The United Nations' Convention on the Rights of the Child ensures the "right of the child to rest and leisure, to engage in play and recreational activities appropriate to the age of the child." If play is a natural instinct, a right and incredibly important in growth development, then why is it that we only encourage it beyond childhood in species other than our own? Dogs are given toys to play with, taken to play dates at the park, and encouraged to romp around and explore well into their senior years. We applaud and even reward most domesticated animals (in the home, zoos, and sanctuaries) for play, yet we're weening our own off of it at younger and younger ages and drop it like a hot potato upon entering adulthood. Why the dichotomous attitude toward play? It is undoubtedly a successful and natural way for people to interact with one another and the world around them, yet for some reason it's only taken seriously during the early childhood phase. Have the stresses of life with standardized testing, homework overload, and social responsibilities rendered play a luxury that only the very young are entitled to? As adults, we not only discourage play in one another but also look down upon it as *childishness*, *immaturity*, and *foolishness*. Time allowed for play in the school day is being cut at an alarming rate, with a shift toward formal academic schooling (and prep for it) starting earlier and earlier. There is now a focus on STEM (science, technology, engineering, and math) being taught to children as young as three years old, and if that weren't enough, there are now droves of programs, movies, and books training to-be parents on how to begin infusing information and knowledge in their babies, even while they're still in the womb!

All of that is not to say that I disagree with educational content being taught to children at young ages. Quite the contrary, I am an advocate for education at every age and on every level. Lifelong learning is a passion of mine, which is why I also believe that play is one of the greatest ways to teach the young and the young at heart. There is a current trend for adults engaging with play, and nothing has done more for this movement than the onset of smartphones with their games and game-based learning apps. Just today I heard two grown men discussing the compelling narrative, stunning artwork, and intricate game mechanics in a particular video game. I'm not a digital gamer myself, be it on a console or an app, but the majority of adults whom I know who play games play them on a digital device. The winds of change are blowing, and play—or more modernly coined, GAMIFICATION—has taken hold of the business world, and it is flourishing. The term "gamification" is fairly new to our vocabulary, first breaking into the scene in 2005, but it is exactly how it sounds—to incorporate game mechanics and theories to nongame environments and/or activities. You've probably encountered this phenomenon without even realizing it.

Do you know the small digital plant on the dashboard of the Toyota Prius cars? The one where you can grow, or add, more leaves by driving more eco-consciously? Car companies, the Environmental Protection Agency, or activist groups can spend billions of dollars in marketing to tell you to lower your carbon footprint by driving at a more sustainable speed, accelerating at a slower pace, or to avoid idling, but for many drivers all of that information was just in one ear and out the next. By turning it into a game, however, via a small digital plant that you're in charge of growing, Toyota has succeeded in getting people to drive more sustainably, not necessarily because they're worried about their carbon footprint but because they're motivated by the game mechanics and are trying to "grow" their plant.

Gamification is rampant in mobile apps, covering every field imaginable. Want to learn a new language? Duelingo teaches you a new language with the feel of a handheld game interface. Need help getting your to-do list done? With Habitica, you can accumulate coins, shop medieval markets, and grow your own menagerie of animals by accomplishing daily tasks. The list for gamified apps that cater to adults goes on and on, and it's only getting longer by the day. Businesses are bringing in game-coaches to help gamify goals; teachers are using game strategies to help explore a variety of topics, and libraries are now joining in on the fun.

Before I get into how to implement play, or gamification, at your library, take a moment to contemplate the word "play." What visual and linguistic associations do you have with that word? Are you transported back to your childhood? Do you think of board games, sports teams, or the jungle gym? What is the most recent memory you have of playing?

Was it with a child, an online game, or a group of adults? In the following space, write down your own definition of and word associations with the word "play."

I'm going to go out on a limb here and suggest that, unless you're an avid gamer or have young children of your own, you probably have to think back to childhood to conjure up an image of what play is and how it relates to your life. In a short survey I conducted with 50 adults, over half of them said that they immediately associated playing with their childhood. In fact, several of the participants became visibly uncomfortable when I asked them the last time that they played. What message does this type of behavior send to our children? That playing is childish and something to be embarrassed about once you reach adulthood?

Our good friends over at the *Oxford Living Dictionary* define play as to "engage in activity for enjoyment and recreation rather than a serious or practical purpose." On the same note, Dictionary.com says to play is "to exercise or employ oneself in diversion, amusement or recreation." These two definitions cover a broad range of what could qualify as play, yet what I am proposing to use play for stands in direct opposition to these definitions. Unlike the dictionary or the modern school-day schedule, I believe that life cannot—and should not—be compartmentalized. The majority of school systems break down their day according to subjects. You have x amount of time per day for math, x amount for reading, x amount for physical fitness, and so on and so forth. One of the "compartments" for the daily schedule, though less and less time is devoted to it each year, is recess—or play. Some might consider the physical education class as falling under the play umbrella, and when dodgeball or soccer is involved, then yes, I can agree. But running the mile, doing sit-ups, and lifting weights are not my idea of enjoyment or amusement. This brings me to another point.

Play is subjective. Much like I despised the chin-up in middle school physical education, many of my peers found it thrilling, all the more so since we were timed and graded right there on the spot in front and center for all the class to see. It was their idea of a game, or play, and more power to them. Many students (myself included) had a running game all throughout middle school, which was dependent upon teachers saying a selected word each day (think Pee Wee's Secret Word). It was a ridiculous game, but it brought some enjoyment to the monotony of the chopped up portions of math, science, reading, and history. Once the last school bell rings, life goes on in an integrated manner. When children visit the playground, they aren't exposed to sunshine for 30 minutes, then fresh air for 30 minutes, and then the swings for 30 minutes. Everything is integrated and happens, more or less, simultaneously. Once these children reach the working age, they will be required to accomplish tasks that necessitate math, critical thinking, writing, problem solving, and so on, all within one project and one time frame. As libraries, we can adopt an integrated mind-set and help better prepare young people to be productive members of society by recognizing and balancing all the components that go into one activity/assignment/experience. We'll get more into this concept in Chapter 7. Until then, back to the games!

It's fairly common for teachers to "play a game" with their students, by rewarding the class for good behavior, high test scores, and the like. Once a certain amount of rewards have been collected (marbles in a jar, stickers on a chart, etc.), the group is given a prize (pizza party, movie day). The problem with this type of "game" is that it is stripped of all strategy and excitement. Essentially, it is not a game at all; rather it is just pure motivation. Score well on the test and be rewarded. It's little more than the system already in place; score well and receive praise and a high grade.

What does play look like in your library? Are there games offered for patrons to use? Do you have an early literacy space where toys are laid out for young children to interact with? Are there video games and consoles available for in-house use? Perhaps you don't even have supplies but rather have a playful attitude and mind-set that bubbles over onto your patrons and ignites a sense of play in them. This lighthearted mind-set is contagious and will help to foster a learning playground.

Free Play versus Structured Play

Let's take it back to early childhood development for a quick minute and unpack the two most prevalent types of play: free and structured. Free play is an unorganized time for play of any sort to take place. Role-play, play with objects such as blocks, toys, and so on, or solitary play can all take place during free play. Think of recess time in the school yard. Everyone is playing, yet the choice to play your own way is the driving force. On the flip side of this, we have structured play: board games, team sports, hide-and-seek. Play where there are rules to be followed and a clearly defined goal to accomplish.

From my own experience working with children in a variety of settings, free play tends to dominate with the younger kids, while structured play is what the older students are drawn to. This makes sense as the younger children have not yet developed the cognitive skills needed for complex game mechanics such as risk, resource management, and strategy. Young children explore the world around them by mimicking and acting out their own scenarios based on what they've seen unfold in front of them (think playing "house"). As they progress, their free play may incorporate more and more self-imposed rules and/or regulations, transitioning the activity into a structured game. As children, my siblings and I had a long-running game we made up, where we were all witches searching for the perfect recipe for our brew. Rules were instated to regulate what was and what wasn't allowed into the cauldron, in addition to what powers each of us had and how they were to be used. This was an activity that started out as free play but morphed as we got older and more complex and engaged ourselves into an organized and thought-out game. Whether it's free play with blocks set up in the literacy center or a structured group scavenger hunt, libraries have many opportunities to engage their patrons with play. Group story times can be turned into a playground by having kids go on visual safari trips on the hunt for shapes, colors, or (if you've had some prep time) hidden figures. I frequently will use pieces from flannel stories or extra puppets and hide them around the room for these types of safaris. The kids are all asked to stay seated and to verbally give me directions to find the hidden object. *It's on the wall!* What wall? *That one!* The FRONT, SIDE, or BACK wall? *The BACK WALL!* By having the kids use verbal cues, they are working on their literacy skills as well as their observation, direction, and creative skill sets, not to mention that they have a ball going "on safari."

At the Free Library of Philadelphia (FLP) the group of children that came to the library on a daily basis much preferred to partake in free play, steering clear of anything that resembled the structure from which they had just been released (school). They opted to play with the open-ended KEVA Planks, LEGOs, or puppets rather than the board games and puzzles that I had set out. With the school day being so rigid, free play (in my observation) was not only a welcome relief for these students but also a release of their creative energy. The imaginations of young people are oftentimes the driving force behind the way in which they play and interact with the world around them.

One day, several months into the school year, a new girl showed up at the library during the after-school hours. Her mother was using the library's computers to work on her college degree, and the young girl would sit at the computers and stare at us over in the children's area. On the very first day she came in, I approached her and invited her to come and join the group of other kids. She was painfully shy, and though she was older (third grade), she didn't want to leave her mom's side. I respected that and let her be.

She and her mother came in just about every day for a week and made a beeline straight to the computers. I always made sure to acknowledge them when they walked in, saying "hello" and giving them a big smile.

One day, they showed up before any of the other kids had gotten there, and the young girl came and sat at the table I was working at. I greeted her and asked how her day was going and got no response. That's okay. Some kids don't like to talk. I got out some LEGOs and began piecing them together at the table. I wasn't making anything in particular, but I moved the spare bricks to be within her reach and encouraged the young girl to help me build. Reluctantly, she obliged. I grabbed a couple small LEGO people (police officers) and began "talking" with them, making up a story of how a big bag of money had been robbed and the police had no leads. The young girl was hooked.

I continued acting out this made-up story, bringing in more and more LEGO people as the girl began to giggle and then laugh aloud. After a few minutes of me, essentially playing by myself, she joined in the fun, grabbing her own LEGO person and contributing to the story. We went on the hunt together and recovered the big bag of money. "What would you do with a big bag of money?" I asked her. "Easy," she replied immediately. "I'd buy an ice-cream truck." I continued asking her questions about the food truck (*What flavors would you have? What's your favorite flavor? If you could invent a flavor, what would it be?* etc.) all the while she was building her truck out of LEGOs. Once she had built it, complete with two axles, four wheels, a windshield, and a light saber, for protection, the other kids had shown up.

They thought her truck was so cool, and after I handed out some fake money that we used for math counting (leftover money from a Monopoly set), they all used it to "purchase" an ice-cream cone of their choice from the truck. After accumulating a good pile of cash, the young girl built a second truck and hired a driver to go out and sell more ice cream. Their imaginations had taken over, and they were steeped in their own world of make-believe, all the while they were heavily engaged in engineering (with the construction of the LEGO food trucks) and with the dreaded *M* word "math"—money transactions used for ice-cream cone purchases, handing out change, adding up costs for more than one cone, discounted flavors that weren't selling well, and so on. Observation and communication skills were being honed as they bartered for their cone prices and simulated mini business transactions. They had inadvertently worked in educational concepts to their free play, and they were having so much fun they didn't even notice that they were also learning and sharpening their skill sets.

When it was time to designing the spy club, I created a skeleton made up of structure-based play that allowed for free play and inquiry-based learning to take place within. This meshing of both forms of play enabled me to control a large group of students at a time while also appealing to the students' desire to be in charge and lead the way. Inquiry-based learning is another key concept in creating exciting programs for your patrons that are also educational. This theory revolves around the idea of the students leading the way, driven by their own inquiry. For example, if you're hosting an event about monsters of the deep sea, rather than standing in front of the group and spouting out facts about spider crabs, angler fish, and gulper eels, you would provide a brief introduction, direct the kids to some resources, and let their imaginations take over. If they start to inquire about the types of equipment used to go down into the seas and explore these unsightly monsters, then the program shifts gears and becomes about the mechanics behind engineering and constructing submarines and scuba gear. The benefit of this teaching approach is that it lends itself to the natural progression of thought and allows for said progression to reach fruition. The downfall to this is that you have to be able to bend and shift with each new direction taken. There is a middle ground available where inquiry is still king but in a controlled manner. More on this is in Chapter 3.

In the applications for agency with the Free Library of Philadelphia Espionage Agency (FLPEA), all of which were signed by the agents, they promised to uphold the FLP values of respect and excellence. This terminology was vague enough to cover everything from bullying to cheating and was what I referred to when I occasionally had to handle disruptive behavior. I held the kids to these same standards even on days that weren't "spy days," when they were "undercover" as regular library patrons working on their homework and playing with the games and toys on offer. If someone began complaining about their homework, or I saw them copying another student's work, then I was quick to remind them of the responsibility that I and the FLP had entrusted to them, encouraging them to live up to the high standards that I know they're capable of. This signed pledge, a code of honor really, gave structure to our spy game and helped to keep kids in line without giving them a rigid set of rules to memorize and follow.

In the spy curriculum, there was an overarching storyline with weekly "chapters" that needed to be followed in sequential order. If a mission wasn't completed, or a corner was cut, then the story was thrown out of order and the subsequent missions were rendered moot. The weekly missions had to be completed, submitted to headquarters, and followed in sequence (structure); the way in which the agents chose to complete the missions, however, was entirely up to them (free play). Allowing the kids to choose their own alias created this alter ego that was brought to life, or released from their mind's eye, on Tuesday afternoons. The kids were so steeped in the story of their spy personas and the world of the FLPEA that they regularly engaged in free play via role-playing different spy scenarios outside of the club, where they were called upon to solve a variety of cases.

The Benefits of Learning through Play

Albert Einstein is often misquoted as saying that "play is the highest form of research." He along with a slew of other people did say something along these same lines, but regardless of this I do believe the sentiment to be true. Play allows for a natural progression of thought and fosters an organic learning process. Let's look outside of our species to big cats. When a mother cat is teaching her cubs how to hunt for food, she does it by playing with them. They mimic the crouch, pounce, and attack with her, which for those of us watching from a safe distance looks an awful lot like playing—because it is! Game mechanics are used to teach dogs, sea lions, and just about any other trainable animal. Many of us learned very basic life skills via games when we were children. Most of us can control our bladders and know how to properly use a toilet, thanks to positive reinforcements (rewards) given to us as children when we opted for the bathroom over the aisle A in the grocery store to relieve our bowels. We know the 26 letters of our English alphabet because of a song we were taught to sing along with. Learning through play is natural, and as an added bonus when we're playing, be it free-form or structured, our brains release dopamine, the feeling of being motivated and doing well. Pairing game mechanics and play theories to teaching concepts will allow for a more positive attitude toward learning and increase chances of comprehension and retention.

The more I focused on playing at my FLP branch, the higher my participation numbers were. For Halloween, I threw a party for the students that promised to have "ghoulish games galore" for the kids to play in their costumes. Initially, the teens were to have their own party in the basement, while the K–5th-graders were upstairs at the kids' party. However, upon seeing the pumpkin bowling alley and sticky spider web game setup, not only did I get the teens participating in the games, but adults also stepped in and played. It was one of the biggest days (number wise) that we had at that branch, and it revolved around playing. Though this was a holiday party and was meant to be a break from the day-to-day educational goals of this after-school program, the kids, teens, and adults all learned about physics as they tried to bowl the lopsided pumpkin down the alley to knock over the ghosts (pins made up of cereal boxes covered in white paper with faces drawn on). "Why won't this pumpkin roll straight?" screeched an exasperated child. "It's not round!" responded another, grabbing the pumpkin to show him how uneven it was. The two worked together to figure out the best angle and speed to roll the pumpkin. They were having so much fun that they didn't even realize that what they were doing was exploring the concepts of physics.

There's a curious change that happens in children around the ages of 8 to 10. The desire to draw, color, or to engage in imaginative play drastically slows down. This also happens to be around the same time that many of these kids begin to slow their personal reading habits. Are these different activities, or the lack thereof, connected in any way? Could it be that the less we read about other people and worlds, the less we're inclined to create our own? As libraries, we're given the unique opportunity to incorporate play on a large scale while also encouraging reading and lifelong learning habits.

Almost every library that I have visited and/or worked in has provided toys for open-ended and free-form play, blocks, puppets, dolls, and so on. But, the thing is that they're usually geared toward the very young. There's nothing wrong with this; in fact, it serves a very real and important need, but open-ended play is also something that your older patrons can participate in as well. Things along the lines of KEVA Planks (small wooden planks used for building), LEGOs, or marbles can all help to kick-start the imagination in, as well as collaboration among, children, teens, and even adults. Sometimes it's not a matter of *what* you have available to play with, but rather *who* feels welcome to participate. By modeling a playful attitude yourself, by interacting with the materials and/or games you have set out, children and teens will follow suit and be more inclined to participate.

A few weeks ago, during one of my evening shifts at the library, I was approached by a six-year-old boy, let's call him M. He told me that his father was busy working on paperwork and was curious about what kind of games I had for him to play. Seeing that he didn't have any siblings to play with, I suggested some memory games that he could play by himself. No, he wasn't interested in those. Upon seeing Uno, however, his eyes lit up, and he told me that that was his favorite game. He begged me to play with him, and since it was later in the evening and most families had already left for the day, I agreed. We played several rounds (he was a terrible cheat, changing the rules and making things up as he went), and he finally lost interest. Putting the cards back, he stumbled upon the chess set and asked if I would play that with him. Despite his cheating nature, I wish I could have spent the entire night playing games with him, but I did have work to do and so suggested that he see if there was anyone else for him to play with. I went and did a quick walk-through in the department and noticed that there was another young boy playing digital chess on one of the computers. Excitedly, I went and grabbed M and told him to follow me. "Excuse me," I said to the boy on the computer, "I notice that you're playing Chess. This is my friend M and we were wondering if you'd like to play a *real* game of chess with him?" He agreed immediately, and off the two boys went. Two hours later, when we were getting ready to close for the day, the boys were on about their sixth round and still chatting away discussing the strategies each was using to play and talking about everything from school to their favorite foods.

The structured play that dictates a game of chess was a perfect way for these two boys to learn about social skills as well as the various concepts behind the complex mechanisms of the game. Though they were only six and seven years old, and couldn't verbalize the theories they were exploring, they were learning nonetheless, all while making a new friend and having fun. Had I just introduced the two boys to one another without anything for them to bond over, the friendship would have had a slower start and less chance of lasting. Playing a game together gave them some common ground to start their friendship with, and they built up on their own relationship from there.

At the beginning of most of the small-scale (under 40 participants) programs that I host for children, I start off with an icebreaker or a quick game. This is designed to bond people quickly giving a chance for the participants to learn a thing or two about one another. This way of learning, by pairing it with a game, is far more effective than having myself read aloud the names of those involved and introducing them all verbally. By offering games and a playful environment, libraries can be a welcome relief from the stresses of daily school life, as well as offering up a new way to look at how we interact with information and knowledge. Students may read and/or be lectured about the engineering required to build a bridge, yet by having bricks or Popsicle sticks available, the students can play and explore the same concepts and theories but in a hands-on and stress-free way. Without having to focus on passing a test, kids are free to explore, design, and build their own bridges. By offering them language to verbalize the concepts they're interacting with, you can bridge the gap between their playing and their school work.

On the flip side, by offering programs that are based on structure, you are providing a framework for students to build upon with their studies. Coding classes are a popular trend that fall into the structured play category. Students (typically the older end of the K–12 spectrum) come to the library for a set amount of time and learn how to use code to create an end product. Many of these end products are a short, choppy version of a video game, but it's something viable that the kids can point to at the end of the program and say, "I made that!"

When creating programs that incorporate play, it forces *you* to play. Either by testing out the coding programs and games or building an example castle for the kids to be inspired by, when you play, it will create connections.

> **Reflection Questions**
>
> 1. What type of play is most prevalent at your library? Free or structured?
> 2. What type of play are you most comfortable with? Free or structured?
> 3. In what ways do you incorporate play into your day-to-day life?

CHAPTER 2

A Perfect Location for Learning

Libraries Are a Safe Space

*The only thing that you absolutely have to know,
is the location of the library.*

—Albert Einstein

I am fully aware that this chapter may be preaching to the choir; nevertheless please humor me as I gush about why libraries are the perfect setting for learning. Aside from the painfully obvious, that reading is a powerful way to gain knowledge, libraries offer up unique ways for people to engage with information. But, before we talk about how children can learn in the library, let's discuss what brings them there in the first place. On a very practical level, libraries—as buildings—are safe spaces. This is a loaded phrase, *safe space*, and I mean it in every sense of the word. In many communities the library is a safe building to take refuge in. Whether it's seeking shelter from the elements, from the streets, or from an abusive home, libraries are a welcoming place for all. This sense of safety has brought in, and will bring in, people from the community who have no intention of "learning" or reading; they're there just to weather the storm and then be on their merry way. Many children will seek out libraries because entry is free of charge and they need somewhere to go from the time school gets out until their guardians get home from work. This gap that we're talking about is typically the 3:00 to 6:00 p.m. time frame, and not coincidentally it is during this time that juvenile crime and violence spikes. Aside from the occasional book thief, libraries stand as a crime and violence-free pillar of hope for those seeking safety. Much like a bookend, the branch that I worked for in the Philadelphia system capped the end of a strip mall and was what we referred to as a "destination library." If you went to the library, it was because you meant to go there. This was not the type of library that you just popped into on your walk home. With that being said, many of the children in my program (some as young as 6) would take city buses from their school to the library—all on their own. Their home wasn't open to them until their parent arrived sometime in the evening, and so, armed with a dollar or two to buy snacks with at the dollar store, they were on their own to fend for themselves. The Free Library of Philadelphia (FLP) has worked hard to maintain a good rep with the community, and a big part of that is giving the people a sense of safety within their walls. Buildings are staffed with security personnel, and they work hard to keep the peace. Children, teens, and adults count on the library to be their refuge, in what can be a tough and cruel world.

Another way to interpret the term *safe space* is the freedom to fail. School systems have very little wiggle room when it comes to the end results, or quantification of learning. You either pass or fail, receive an A or a B, you get it or you don't. Classrooms are becoming more and more crowded, and our poor teachers are tasked with the impossible charge to move them all from point A to point B in X amount of time. Simple math tells us that when the variables (children) increase, so does the chance for failure. With 30 first-graders, you have 30 different learning levels and styles: someone is going to struggle; someone is going to fail. When a child fails in school, he or she faces several ramifications: possible criticism from his or her teachers, ridicule from peers, and poor grades to name just a few. Failure in school is equated with a lack of intelligence, which is incredibly unfair. Einstein summed this dilemma up perfectly when he said that "everybody is a genius. But if you judge a fish by its ability to climb a tree, it will live its whole life believing that it is stupid." Libraries offer safety to children because without a structured learning system in place with regimented testing, they are free to learn, do, and create at their own pace and in their own way. Failure is now an option, because there aren't any ramifications. While working with my group of kids at the FLP, I was amazed at how many of them believed that not only were they not smart but they had also come to the conclusion that they couldn't learn. They had failed so many times at school that it was now an expectation. In that vein, working with them on homework was akin to pulling teeth—in fact, several of them would probably have opted for the teeth-pulling over completing their take-home sheets. As the librarian, whether you—or the children—realize it or not, you are a role model for all who enter your space. The language (both with your body and your words) is fully noted and can be used to make others feel threatened—or to make others feel safe. Unless you're screaming like a banshee from the moment patrons walk into the building, your body language is what's going to be seen/interpreted first. Many of us sit behind a desk, guarded by our computer monitors, but the way you sit and present yourself can covey meaning. Arms folded, head down, a scowl, and a frown are all extremely uninviting. Sitting up with good posture (I know, I know, I need to work on this too), arms open, looking up at patrons, and a smile on your face tell people that they are welcome, that you enjoy where you are (and so too can they), and that there is a sense of safety (i.e., you're not afraid, so they shouldn't be either). When not behind the desk and talking with patrons, keep the same thing in mind. Open body language equals a feeling of welcomeness. In Chapter 3, we'll dive into a more detailed look at how your body language affects your message, but for now make these simple changes a part of your daily habit and see what a difference it will make. Open body language and a smile will go a very long way; this I promise you—but we cannot stop there. The words we use with others, especially children, have a big impact. To help ensure that your space is safe it is imperative that language be considered. As a child, my family and I were collectively banned from our local public library. Admittedly, we had terrible difficulty getting anything returned on time, and one day when we went to check out our favorite movie, *The Birdcage*, along with any Beverly Cleary and Roald Dahl we could get our hands on, the librarian (not so kindly) let us know that we were no longer welcome to use her fine and quiet institution. Our library cards were voided and my siblings and I were instilled with a sense of shame and a fear of libraries and their gatekeepers. Miraculously, I made it all the way until my freshmen year in undergrad without going to a public library and with very little interaction with the elementary/middle/high school librarian. To this day, though we're all grown adults now, my siblings still won't set foot in a library (though they fully applaud my work in and for libraries). All that to say, the language the librarian used toward us as a children left a deep and ugly scar. We all have the option to use positive or negative words in every interaction we have. I encourage you to challenge yourself to try and speak only in positive words. Rather than telling a rogue child to "Get down from that shelf, and for the love of Pete—PUT YOUR PANTS BACK ON!," perhaps we can spin it and say, "I'd love to help you reach that book you're climbing toward, and though your blue pants look great on our carpet I bet they would look even better on your legs!" This is an extreme example, but I trust you get my point. This challenge may sound simple, but believe you me, this can tax even the most easygoing and positive-speaking public librarian! When it comes to using language in programming for our library, I try and keep the same positive-only language thing going. Failure can be a very sensitive issue for many children, and for some, it can be a barrier to participation. Ensuring the children that there is no wrong answer is paramount, and since I do not implement any official testing, it is easy to eliminate closed questions and open the floor up to open-ended questions. When identifying the continents on a world map I had some children point to Africa and say it was Mexico. Instead of telling them right off of the bat that they were wrong, I asked what they knew about Africa and Mexico. After talking among themselves they deduced that the continent in question could not be Mexico because (a) Mexico, one realized, was a country, not a continent, and (b) Mexico was close to the United States. We looked closer at the map and with a few hints (giraffes and gorillas are native to this land) they were able to correctly identify it as Africa. Not only did we use positive language in this activity but we also learned about Africa in addition to learning about Mexico, giraffes, and gorillas. Your own language is not the only language you must be aware of. Bullying is real, and it is something that I do not tolerate in the slightest. Whether I'm at the reference desk, leading a program, or asking for a third glass of hard cider (I do work in public libraries after all), I am on the lookout for and prepared to attack against bullying. Everyone has his or her own way of dealing with bullying, on broad library-wide levels down to their own personal level. Know what your library states as acceptable behavior and use that to back you up. Also, it's important to know how you personally will deal with bullying. Role-play is a great way to discover that either you're very comfortable with confrontation or that you freeze up and lose all train of thought. Know your place of work's stance on bullying (both verbal and physical), know your own stance, and then have an action plan. Post rules in your programming areas if need be. Personally, I do not post rules, but opt for a group discussion before a program begins.

I briefly explain that in order to participate in the program and that in order to succeed in life (I try and make as many connections with the outside "real" world as possible—more on this in Chapter 6), positive language is a must. Most kids I've come in contact with are all about the freedom to be themselves without having to worry about being teased, so in turn they do not tease others and are quick to call out those who do. This preprogram chat helps build in a self-regulating anti-bully system, meaning the kids keep each other in check and then when they can't moderate their own issues they ask me for intervention.

The vibe that you give off as the leader of your programs at the library will have an immediate and lasting impact. To encourage children to learn is one of my main, if not *the* main, goals I have when creating programs, and a safe environment free of violence and the freedom to fail are essential in accomplishing that. We all have the choice to give off light in this dark world, but it takes active empathy and participation. Please, for the sake of the public, don't let your Voldemort out and scare the patrons off. Shine your glorious book-filled light and be the magic that kids read and dream about.

When creating a program for your patrons, go over the following questions to ensure that your environment is a safe space.

Is your building secure?

Are you familiar with safety and emergency procedures?

Are you comfortable in your space?

Is failure encouraged in your space?

Does your body language reflect a warm and welcoming space?

A Library Reflects the Culture in Which It Lives

When meeting library staff, as well as other public servants, I'm always interested in learning whether or not they're from the community in which they serve. In my case, the answer is most often no, as I'm quick to pick up and move when an opportunity arises. I'm a wanderer at heart and stand out as such in most places I travel to, but there was no place I stuck out more than in Philadelphia. I, being a white Midwesterner—specifically a Chicagoan (CHI-KAH-go-AHN)—did not reflect the language culture, the food culture, the historical culture, or the majority of the racial culture of the community in which I served. People were quick to pick up on this, as my heavy Chicago accent was a giant red flag. One day, shortly after I started working at the FLP, I was helping an adult patron when she accused me of being foreign to Philly because my "vowels go all the way up to the ceiling and back." I never had my accent been described as such, but I laughed and agreed with her that my vowels do indeed stretch a little higher and longer than hers did. Because I was so obviously not a Philadelphian, or an East Coaster, it took me a while to gain the community's trust. However, because I was endorsed by the FLP—an institution that greatly reflects its community and is held in high regard—I had an "in" which expedited the "trust transition." The library was held in high regard with the greater Philadelphia community, and so I was credited with the same confidence, if merely by association. This is not to say that the kids, or even some of the adults, trusted me right away. There was still about a six-week period where I had to prove that I was going to stick around, that I knew what I was doing, and that I cared about the well-being of these kids. Once the kids and I had passed the first rounds of major school testing in October, I threw them a Halloween party. I could feel the trust between us building up. Do your patrons, of all ages, trust you? Do they feel comfortable with you? Are you accessible and willing to help? These types of questions are constantly rolling through my mind, as I'm continuously welcoming new faces to my current library.

A few years back I had the opportunity to spend six months in Turku, Finland (look it up, it's a real place, I promise), and their library was my lifesaver. I arrived at the tail end of what was a brutal and dark winter. The sun was starting to make a, albeit short, daily appearance after about six months of complete darkness, while the solid Aura River started to slowly split and return to its liquid state. With little to do outside and not knowing more than a handful of Finnish words, I found myself taking refuge in the public library. It was a beautiful reflection of the culture I had been thrown into and a good introduction to the community I was about to experience, as the longer and warmer days drew out the locals and the festivities began. Turku's artists' work lined the walls, people of all sorts roamed the aisles, displays illustrated the town's tumultuous history with Russia, and the librarians helped me ease into a life totally and utterly foreign to me. After searching for the grocery store for three days (and living off of Hesburger—fast-food joint, for that entire time), it was a librarian who directed me to the hidden escalator in the perfume section of the mall that leads to the basement where the grocery store is located (because that makes sense). It was the librarians who gave me the best recommendations for restaurants and cafes, and who helped me discover a town for which I now hold dear to my heart. The librarians were not only information experts; they were also culturally aware of the community in which they served and lived, and were eager to help me integrate into it. So, what does all of this have to do with libraries being a perfect setting for learning? As a foreigner to Finland, it helped me tremendously to know that I had a place to go whether it was to ask for the translation of a Finnish word comprising of 45 letters, 2 of which were vowels (this may be a slight exaggeration, but only *slightly*), or to ask why people walked around with bags of bread tied to their belts (turns out, if you've got food on your person, then that allows for public drinking) or to ask for the Finnish word for "floor soap," having unsuccessfully mimed my way through three stores looking for the stuff, all the while inadvertently offending a handful of people (still not sure what it was that set them off). The library was my safe space and a perfect setting to learn about my new neighbors.

As a foreigner to Philadelphia and before I was hired by the FLP, one of the first things I did after moving there was to get a library card. The various branches were a great way for me to assimilate to my new home, as I got a feel for the different neighborhoods and was able to read up on the quirks that make Philly stand out. I quickly learned what the *Wawa* was (gas station), how to tell the difference between a *grinder* and a *hoagie*, and where to get the best tomato pie. For people who are not foreign to the community, the library can be a place of pride for it's a reflection of them, their neighbors, and their world. Culture is its own capital and it is highly valuable. Local artists whose works decorate the walls can serve as a lesson on artistic interpretation, among many other things. Local clubs that come and use the library as their venue for meetings can help to start and maintain conversations that matter and lead to transformative change. In many lessons taught whether it be math or science, an infusion of empathy can be added by incorporating culture to the equation. Rather than dryly mapping out a math problem, 20×3, let's say, how much more impactful it would be if we infuse some culture and change the script. If Philadelphia has 20 artists and they are all asked to carve three different statues of Philly's very own Benjamin Franklin, how many Bens will we have to place around town? Too many, but you get my point. Healthy library will be one that interacts with its patrons on several levels. The collections will represent a wide variety of user interests, displays will reflect the people walking in the doors, staff will know how to appropriately interact with diverse crowds, and programs will appeal to the masses. It's important to be a genuine reflection of not only your patrons but also your community as a whole. When trying to get more foot traffic and new people in the doors, it's important to remember that if people don't see themselves in the books, on the shelves, or in the hallways, then they are less likely to show up and/or make return visits. From creating displays that show a variety of people groups to incorporating different world languages in programs, you can take small steps to become a place that reflects the commonwealth in which your library is rooted. A simple way that I do this is by welcoming my family story times with multiple languages. "Hello!" "Jambo!" "Hola!" "Namaste!" If it's a manageable sized group, I'll ask for volunteers to say "hello" in their native tongue. This gives kids who speak multiple languages a chance to show off their skills, showcase their culture, and play the role of teacher/informer as they coach us all in how to say their greeting. By recognizing cultural diversity in your groups through simple activities like this, you can let people know that they're seen and that they're welcome in your space. It's a simple activity that takes less than two minutes, but one that can have a lasting impact and can help to shine a light on our cultural diversity. Books tend to be heavy-handed when it comes to stories about white children, and even more so when it comes to the cover art. We have a disproportionate amount of white authors and illustrators in the kid lit world; however, by purchasing books about and by people of color and showcasing them in your displays, you'll send a message of inclusivity and a global mind-set. Reflecting your own community is a vital part in creating a rich learning environment, but you mustn't stop there. Don't just cater to and showcase the cultures represented in your zip code. If you have a global mind-set when creating and implementing programs, then you'll be modeling and encouraging your young participants to think globally as well. It has been scientifically proven that stories help to create empathy, and by modeling a celebration of differences, you'll only be reinforcing the powerful lessons kids are learning between the pages of their favorite books. The world we live in is becoming smaller and smaller every day, and by giving our young patrons a wide-lens angle of the microcosm in which they live, we can help them to become global citizens. If you have a deep understanding of where you come from and what your town and its society are like, the easier it will be to look out and explore other communities and the way in which they work. While the school is another great place for students to be exposed to the diverse peoples that they are neighbors with, the library opens the door a bit further for not only are kids interacting with other kids, but people of all ages, abilities, and from all walks of life come in and use the library. It's a perfect setting for learning about the world around us in a small and compact way. Culture and knowledge go hand in hand, and where better for the two to flourish than within the walls of a public library? Books, computers, staff, patrons, and the personalities that they all bring to the table help libraries foster an environment ripe with possibilities.

Books, Computers, Staff, and Patrons Are All Excellent Resources

Librarians are tasked with the wonderful charge of creating collections that reflect and satisfy their patrons. This diversity of texts is not only beneficial to the patrons, but it can also be fuel for your programming fire. Want to do a program on dinosaurs? The first place to go is your dinosaur collection. Need an idea for a program? Take a look and see which books have a high circulation count and check for repeating themes/genres. Are your books on paper airplanes flying out the door (pun intended)? Then perhaps an airplane innovation workshop is in order. You could also look at your collections in the opposite light. Which books are not circulating well? Has it been a while since the earth science books were looked at? Perhaps an exciting program on extreme weather or extreme geography will pique interest and increase circulation of those texts. When I find myself needing to plan a program with a rather quick turnaround, I tend to head to the nonfiction stacks and browse the aisles until a topic grabs my attention (most recently this was a book on the Earth's layers) and then I go from there. For more involved and thought-out programming I have a different technique for selecting my topic/theme, more of which we'll get into in Chapter 3. Once you've got your theme for your program selected, the books you have in your collection are your first sources for research. The beauty of working in a library is that it's made for learners of all ages. You as a program developer can research the Crab Nebula with books found in the adult nonfiction collection, and then turn around and have age-appropriate juvenile books to show and/or check out to those who attend your nebula program. Authors put a whole lot of work into creating the beautiful books you've got on your shelves, so take advantage of them and incorporate them in your planning and programming. As of March 2017 more than half of the world's population still doesn't have access to the Internet. A good many people who do have access rely on public computers to connect them to the World Wide Web, and so off to the library they go. In both library systems that I've worked for, kids coming to the library make a beeline straight to the computers to play games. This is a point of contention with many; however, time spent online at the library may be the only access to the digital world that these kids have. Rather than telling them that they need to spend less time in front of the screen and more time reading books, we can help them to develop good online habits. Your computers, paired with the Internet, are an incredibly valuable resource that helps contribute to the excellent learning environment of libraries. Access to databases for school research projects, or, for the inquisitive mind, dual language learning software, educational games, and much more are all very good and well and should be encouraged in the library. For your programming, take a look at how these online and digital game developers formulate their stories and take note. Become familiar with the games that these kids are playing. By familiarizing yourself with your young patrons' Internet/computer habits, you can begin to build an excellent pool of references for your own program development. What is the storyline behind the video game these kids play? What are the game mechanics employed in these games? *Storytelling? Memory? Trading? Risk management? Strategy? Voting? Teamwork?*

One week during a spy club meeting, we were discussing Morocco as a potential city of refuge for our thief who was still at large. One of the clues given to the young agents was to figure out which library staff member—we'll call him Mr. M—had been to Morocco and then ask them the secret interview question. Our security guard was the one in question, and the kids were all well aware of and familiar with this man. He was the first face they saw upon entering the building and he was sure to greet them each day, bid them farewell each evening, and enforced the no food policy during in between times. The kids all knew his name and could probably give you a spot-on drawing of his face because they saw him so frequently, but they didn't know much else about him. On that day, they all learned that he has served in the U.S. Navy and had sailed around the world, spending some time in Morocco. Here was a person who was filled with stories and knowledge that the kids had no idea about. All it took was a little nudge, and from then on out, he was a rock star to them all. The following week we had a mission that dealt with designing and constructing a boat, and without any input from myself the kids all went and flooded Mr. M with questions about the ships he sailed on and open waters he crossed. Mr. M was able to relive some of his Navy days and use his stories to educate children about everything from nautical flags to

Moroccan culture. We all have a story to tell, and from those stories, we can all learn something new. I encourage you to be more inquisitive with your fellow staff members and patrons. Ask them questions; and get to know them. The quiet and reserved shelver may have lived a life of high adventure while backpacking across Australia. The loud and rambunctious adult librarian may have had a close encounter with death, and from that learned some valuable life lessons that are worthy of passing on to others. We can learn something from everyone if we're willing to listen; the trick is to listen to understand rather than to respond. Pay close attention to those whom you're surrounded by, and base your questions on observations you make. Ask the origin story for that unique tattoo you see on Bob's left arm. When Pam brings in a homemade snack for the staff, ask where she got the recipe from. When Barb suggests hosting a drag queen story time, ask her if she has a favorite drag queen. For all we know, Barb could be a headlining drag king at the local bar who wants to bring the art of drag to the library. Everyone has a unique story that they are living out, and by being inquisitive and genuinely interested in them, you may be blown away by what people will tell you. It's true that the collections and computers enhance the learning environment of any library, but the people are also a big factor in why libraries are such an excellent location to learn in. Each and every person who walks through your doors, staff and patron alike, brings with him or her a unique set of skills, stories, and ideas, all of which are valuable. By fostering connections between patrons and staff, you're helping to instill a learning playground via storytelling. Tech toys, components, and supplies are all needed on a practical level when working with kids, but teaching them to listen to someone else's story is a valuable skill that will benefit them in every aspect of their lives. The ability to listen, *really* listen, to someone else will reinforce patience, communication, and observation skills. Good listeners become good storytellers themselves after they see what works, what doesn't, and what makes up a good story. Storytelling can be beneficial in all walks of life, from marketing agents crafting a story to sell a product to rocket scientists crafting a story that will inspire further exploration of man's space travel. Stories are the oldest way of communicating and of teaching, and they've stood the test of time for a reason. They work; they're effective tools for entertaining, inspiring, and educating. Books, as wonderful as they are, are not the only source for gathering stories. Everyone, every single person, has a story to tell. At any given moment during working hours, libraries are twofold. There is the print library that houses stories written down on paper and bound in books. Then, there is the walking, living library that lives in each of us. Stories are written on our hearts and minds and are bound by the retelling of them. Challenge yourself to be a holistic librarian who can curate excellent and diverse print collections, and recognize and respect the living collections of stories walking through the stacks.

The BIG Picture

You can help establish libraries as the perfect locations for learning by

- fostering a safe space for children where they are free to explore, fail, and grow, all the while feeling supported and valued;
- reflecting the community in which your library lives via books, displays; and programming that is inclusive and tailored to your unique region;
- utilizing the rich resources that surround you from books to databases to patrons and staff.

Reflection Questions

1. How can you make your space feel safer?
2. Are you actively reflecting the faces that walk through your doors with the materials and programming that you provide?
3. Who are TWO people on your staff that you can commit to trying to get to know better?

CHAPTER 3

Getting to Know Your Audience

How to Listen to Children

Now that we've covered what play is and why the library is the perfect location for learning, let's talk shop about how to get to know who your audience is. As you may very well know, listening to children requires a different and very special skill set than is needed when listening to adults. Recently, I was doing story time with a crowd of nearly 150 people. The theme was being sick and/or hurt and noticing that one young girl (maybe five or six years old) was wearing a band-aid on her finger, I went up to her and asked her to tell the group what had happened. About five minutes later, after she had introduced us all to the names of her pets and described the decorations used in her bedroom in great detail (all of which was completely unrelated to the injury), we found out that she had "ripped open her skin." Everything from her odd phrasing of words to describe the injury to the meandering thought process of the events that transpired was unpredictable and jumbled, yet the entire room was rapt with attention, for kids are drawn to band-aids and the stories behind them like moths to flame.

Had I asked someone in the story time group to tell me why they came to the library that day, I would have lost the group entirely. My audience was not interested in why anyone was there, but the majority of them were of the age where band-aids still held magical powers and were to be revered and asked for at the slightest sign of a scratch—or "tear" as my young friend would say.

With children, active listening takes practice and time. If I were to make prolonged eye contact with a stranger (adult, let's say) in line at the grocery store, then I would have most likely reverted to my go-to topic, the weather. *Can you believe this weather we're having?* The conversation would be shallow and very short. Rarely, a friendship will blossom between two adults who meet randomly outside of a party or other social gathering. But with children, this is another story entirely and I believe it's because with kids inhibitions are thrown to the wind, or more accurately, not developed yet.

For a great many of you, this will be elementary and for that I apologize. Nevertheless, what we're about to discuss is important, so grab a big cuppa and get cozy. I've worked hard to develop my communication skills with children, and the very first thing I learned is to have a nonthreatening eye contact. Kids, much like dogs, can look into your eyes and know exactly what mood you're in. I don't mean that they can read your mind—though in some cases this may prove otherwise—but what I mean is that they can instantly tell if you're genuine. Many times I have seen angry adults plaster on a terrifyingly forced smile and through clenched teeth tell the kids that they are "not mad, but would really appreciate if they would turn the noise down a few hundred decibels," or something of that nature. An angry energy is palpable, and kids don't react well to it. They will physically retreat from you, or since every action has an equal and opposite reaction, they may push back against you with a force that will curdle your blood in a matter of seconds.

Let's step back a minute and assume that you are not upset; using warm and inviting eye contact will then be much easier for you. If you've got resting angry eyebrows (as I admittedly do), then make a conscious effort to raise them up and put a smile on. A smile will get you a long way and it helps to ease your eye contact as well. I encourage you to look at your reflection in the mirror, or in windows as you're walking by parked cars and practice using welcoming eye contact (just make sure no one is sitting in the said parked car). You may look silly, but if you're having trouble connecting with children, then this may make a bit of a difference.

Now that you're able to look children in the eye without them retreating, get down to their actual eye level—that is, if you're physically able. If you're not able to kneel on the floor, then that's okay. Just be aware of your body language when talking and listening to children. If you are able to get down to the floor, then try to get on the same eye level as them.

Regarding this, I conducted a small experiment at my library. During one of my four-hour shifts at the children's reference desks, I split up my interactions with children into two modes: the first being seated behind the desk and the second being getting on the same eye level as the child.

I tried both modes of interactions with each child, to see if his or her communication was affected. Spoiler alert! It was. With one young girl, in particular, my point was proven dramatically. The child in question was around four years old and I had never met her before. She was just about as tall as the reference desk, but not yet able to see over it. I saw her walking toward the desk/children's area with her mother and greeted her by commenting on how lovely her tutu complemented her rain boots. She proceeded to twist up into a literal human pretzel while simultaneously shimmying behind her mother's legs. I continued to ask her questions about her outfit, all the while sitting behind the desk and got no response. In fact, she became more flustered with each passing question.

Then I got up, walked around, and knelt on the ground near her. My eyes were at the same two-foot level as hers, and as she lifted her eyes to mine for the first time, she untwisted her body and became more relaxed. I asked her the same questions that she hadn't responded to earlier and she ended up talking my ear off for several minutes. With other children, I repeated the experiment with sitting and then standing, and they too showed signs of being more at ease when I was at their level. When upright, all 5 feet 2 inches of me, I am pretty much at or below the eye level of the 10-plus-year-old patrons. All of this to say, being on children's level is less threatening to them, and that's important to factor in when trying to gain their trust and become a better listener.

In addition to the physical aspects that will help you become a good listener with children, it is also important to show genuine concern for and interest in them. Remember that I said kids can detect what kind of mood you're in? I understand that being a librarian is heavily steeped in customer service and often requires you to put on that facade of happiness, but it's okay to let children know that we're not always having the best of days. Rather than trying to cover it up with a fake smile or empty words (of which kids will pick up on immediately), it may prove to be a great conversation starter to talk about emotions other than happiness that all humans feel at one point or another. If this is uncomfortable for you, then I understand. It's perfectly possible to be having a bad day, yet smile warmly and show kindness to people. When you're listening to the kids, listen to understand, rather than to respond. The type of storytelling that children engage in when they tell you about their day, or their pet snake, or how they tore their skin is a fantastic literacy activity and what better place than a library and what better person than a librarian to tell these stories to?

Have you smelled anything weird lately? This is one of my favorite questions to ask kids who are reluctant to speak with an adult. *Have you seen any bugs today? What did you eat for breakfast? Did you have any dreams last night?* These are all questions that I will ask kids who venture into my vicinity, rather than *How was school today?* or *How are you doing?* I find that those types of questions will get me one- or, if I'm lucky, two-word answers. Asking them out of the ordinary questions catches them off guard, will more often than not make them smile, and get them chatting. If you're feeling adventurous, then give this a go, and the farther out of the box the questions, the better!

It's become a running joke with me that I have a sign on my back that only children can see, and it says *come and talk with me.* I can be absolutely anywhere, and if there's a child in the same vicinity, then he or she will find me and talk to me. Standing in line at an auto mechanic's shop, I was surprised to feel a little hand grab my finger. I looked down to see what was probably a three-year-old boy, and as I knelt down next to him to ask where his parents were, he began to tell me all about his day. I sat and listened, asking occasional questions, all the while keeping an eye out for mom, dad, or some other guardian. After a few moments, his dad came around the corner and apologized profusely, and my new friend and I parted ways. This isn't just the odd occasion; it happens almost every time I leave the house. Kids feel a certain level of comfort with me, and it's not because I'm something special; rather I believe it's because I see them.

It's not realistic to expect to be able to have a great impact on every child and youth that walk through your doors. There simply isn't enough time in the day. That doesn't mean that we shouldn't strive to make those positive impressions, however. Something small that you can do with each child who visits you at your library is let him or her know he or she is seen. This is done simply by making eye contact with and acknowledging their presence. Let them know that they are part of your community and are welcome. If you're able to, get down (or up) to their eye level and show genuine interest in what they have to say. All of these things combined will make you a better listener, but be prepared to hear some off-the-wall banter! After all, "kids say the darnedest things!"

Organized Chaos

With the school day being an organized and regimented block of time, the last thing that children want afterward is more structure. Unfortunately, we do not run zoos, so some structure cannot be helped, but what we *can* help to foster is organized chaos. Even when we're not talking about programs that directly follow the school day (weekends, summer reading, winter break, etc.), kids will still be loud, rambunctious, and a bit chaotic.

As librarians, and informal educators, harnessing and playing to this wildness can be in our favor.

A good deal of how to create this sense of organized chaos is dependent upon the structure of your building. It is completely understandable that children's volume should be curbed if your library has an open-floor plan —meaning, the adult and teen sections are close by and within hearing range. One such library that I worked for had this type of plan, and coming up with a solution for noise control was first on the docket for organizing the chaos. With limited space and no budget, we had to come up with some unique solutions to our noise problem.

I created small subsections of the children's department, with clear boundaries so that the kids knew where they were allowed to get away with what. All free-play games and toys were set up along the back wall behind the DVD racks. This was the space for making noise and very little structure. The only rules were that you had to be respectful of the building, of the toys, and of each other. Within spitting distance were the child-size tables, of which two were strictly for homework, one for the passive makerspace, and one for checking in. Outside of these areas were the books and computers, all of which fell under the Quiet Zone.

As evidenced in the previous section, I will *always* encourage storytelling in a child. It is well known that for most children their volume level increases with their level of excitement. If, for instance, I was in the Quiet Zone of the library and ran into a child who started telling me about how she discovered what she thought was a dinosaur bone while burying and giving the last rites to Douglas, her deceased pet rat, I would do one of two things: (a) start walking in the direction of the children's department and encourage her to follow me or (b) interject affirmations in a quiet and hushed tone. Children will pick up on your behavior and without having to interrupt a speaker and tell them to "take it down a notch . . . or ten" or "use your inside voice," you can encourage them to mimic your own actions while simultaneously encouraging them to continue with their story.

Another way to foster organized chaos is to make your space enticing to children of all ages. Have age-appropriate toys and games out for as many age ranges as you can. I had very few young children (babies and toddlers) visiting the library on a regular basis in Philadelphia; nevertheless there were always stuffed animals and toys of some sort for them to play with. For the older children I had KEVA planks, board games, and a maker cart. The teens had their own space with a few bean bags for lounging in, but were welcome to join me and the other kids at any time. Giving kids a space that is solely devoted to them shows that you acknowledge them and value their existence. This is no small feat, as I've heard stories of libraries wanting to cut children's departments for several reasons—the noise level being one.

There was one staff member in particular at a branch I worked at who was initially upset with the noise level coming from the children's department. He griped, complained, and was quick to issue stern *shush*es. I tried explaining the loud nature of children, but he was not having it. So, I listened to his complaints, and in doing so I learned quite a bit about this person. Here's a pro-tip: people like to talk about themselves, especially if you're willing to listen. This person was ripe with stories, and upon learning (in addition to their dislike of noise) that he had sailed the world with the Navy, I quickly incorporated that into my programming. During one of our spy meetings, the clue was to interview library staff and determine which of them had been to Morocco. When the kids conducted interviews and figured out who the person in question was, they were flabbergasted! Here in their midst, all this time, was a globe-trotter and instantly they idolized him as a rock star! The person in question felt appreciated and valued, and the kids learned something new about the world at large and about this person that they saw on a daily basis. No longer did I hear any rough *shush*ing. In fact, what I heard was this man sharing more stories and even defending the children and their noise level.

Making your space safe is paramount, but making children feel like it's *their* space is key for repeat visits. I had a habit of taping kid's artwork and discarded projects up on the walls, partly to cover up the preexisting gouges in the paint, as well as to show off their creations to the community at large. This made for a beautiful area, and the children took pride in seeing their work up on display. I noticed several kids eagerly inviting their caretakers (who normally stood outside and texted them that they were there and waiting) into the building so they could see their work up on the walls. Our adult librarian had decorated the teens' area with beautiful paintings the teen group had done during a specific program hosted at the library. Our library was a beautiful hodgepodge of things created by children of all ages.

So far we've talked about organizing chaos on a day-to-day basis, or for passive programming. When it comes to special programs, organization requires a bit more thought and planning at your end. When in the planning phase, you must anticipate the thought processes of children and work that into your content. In short, you must think like a kid. For example, during one of our spy club meetings, there was a scavenger hunt for a particular clue. Knowing that kids (at least the ones I was working with) would have a free-for-all running around and tearing through everything, I worked some specific language into the "mission from headquarters." In describing their mission, I emphasized that we were a TOP SECRET agency and that we needed to remain as such. This meant absolutely no running or yelling. Part of the mission was that the kids had to act as if nothing was out of the norm and that they were simply browsing the stacks—definitely not searching for top secret information sent over from an elite espionage agency! The kids ate it up (partly because I sold it to them, more of which we'll discuss in Chapter 7) and successfully were able to search through the library without causing a scene and destroying everyone and everything in the process. I was able to give parameters in a fun way, but still allow for the kids to feel in control of the situation. I organized the chaos.

If you're hosting a program that requires strict rules for safety's sake, then I encourage you to have a mini discussion with the participants about why those rules exist. When I was a teacher for the Houston Zoo, I started each class with a lesson explicitly about the rules. Seeing that our classroom (the zoo) was filled with literal lions, tigers, and bears—oh my!—and my gaggle of 30 six-year-olds were walking snacks for aforementioned animals, rules were pretty darn important. Each time I presented the rules, I encouraged discussions about why there were rules and how we could follow them. *Rule number one: Stay together at all times. Why do you think we need to be together? What would happen if someone got lost?* Invariably, there was always a wisecrack who went off spouting things like, "you'll get eaten by the HIPPOPOTAMUS and then you'll turn into HIPPPO POOP!" It's moments like this that I absolutely love, because the kids are all laughing hysterically ("poop" is an instant icebreaker for six-year-olds) and it's an excellent teaching moment. *Hippos have flat teeth and only eat plants—herbivore so do you think a hippo would really eat you? No. A tiger on the other hand has sharp teeth and eats meat—a carnivore—would they eat you? YES! So, we need to stay together so no one gets lost and turned into tiger poop!*

Thankfully, there are significantly less (though still some) predators and poop to worry about in the public library sphere, so our rules are a little less extreme. Nevertheless, a conversation with the kids about why these rules exist, and allowing for them to come up with the reasons will help them to remember, but more importantly to understand, the rules. Encouraging kids to come up with their own rules is another great way to allow them to feel in control while still having structure. A fringe benefit of having set areas within your department, as well as rules to accompany them, is that this sense of structure will help to build up trust between you and your community. Consistency allows for people to feel secure, to feel stable, and to develop trust.

Gaining the Child's and Family's Trust

If we rewind to the summer of 2007, you'll find me standing in a barn in the middle of the bush in northern South Africa. I've only just arrived for my three-month internship for my undergraduate degree and I've been tasked with helping to look after the farm animals, which included a pregnant sow, a small herd of goats, and a half dozen Dutch war horses. On this particular day, I was being tested to see if I would be a good fit to look after the mammoth equestrians via the "trust test." Those of you familiar with Sandra Bullock movies will recognize this test as the same one Bullock was asked to perform in her movie *28 Days*. To test the level of trust between human and horse, you must rub your hand along the upper haunch and down one of the back legs of the horse, with a goal of coaxing the horse to pick up its foot for you. Despite all the moxie I could muster and the pleads I telepathically sent to my horse, his hoof did not budge and I was relegated to the pigs and goats (both of which I managed to let loose—farming is obviously not my strong suit).

Thankfully, herding children comes to me much easier than herding farm animals. The very first step in gaining trust with your community members is to simply show up to work. The more they see your face, the more at ease they will become with you. Put into practice positive eye contact, welcoming body language, and a welcoming space, and you are well on your way to establishing transformative and impactful relationships with your patrons. For those children and families who shy away from the reference desk, I suggest you go out and meet them where they're at. Don't fall into the trap of using the desk as a defense shield against the public (as enticing as that sounds). Get up and practice your roaming reference, say hi to as many people as you can, and be an overall point of positivity in the library. These things may sound minute and petty, but people notice them and they can have a profound impact.

Gaining the trust of the child requires a different set of skills than that of gaining the trust of the caretakers. Children want to have fun, and your allowance of and interaction with the children and their "play" will speak volumes. Again, I know that the reference desk is an important factor in your day-to-day life, but when given the chance to go and interact with children (outside of planned programming), you can begin to build bridges and get to know your audience better. Think of it this way: If you don't allow for play in your department, or partake in it on a daily basis, then what reason will the children have to believe that the programs you offer will be any different?

On the flip side, if you do interact with children and help to foster a fun environment, then this will benefit you in multiple ways. First, you're transforming the library from a stationary resource center to a living and breathing environment that is fun. The stereotypes of dark, quiet, and stuffy buildings will be blown out of the water. Second, if children have fun with you, then they will be inclined to ask to attend your programs. Third, the children will be your best advertising. Word of mouth is a powerful tool, but it has to be organic and based on true experiences; daily fun with kids can help create this.

When you've won over the hearts of children, then parents are bound to notice. From my own experience, parents are eager to have their children in free programming that (a) the kids enjoy and (b) teaches them something useful (bonus points for teaching something related to the school's curriculum, but more on this in Chapter 6).

Another factor to consider in gaining the child's and family's trust is cultural competence. Are you aware of the unique differences between you and your community members? Are you actively building a collection that accurately reflects the people walking in the doors? Are your programs inclusive to people of all backgrounds? Do you tokenize groups, or only recognize them on particular holidays related to their culture? As our country continuously diversifies, these types of questions are important to keep in mind.

Though it's impossible for us to ever achieve cultural competence, for one cannot possibly become fully competent of a culture to which he or she was not born into, or does not belong, it is important to strive to get as close as we can. Studies have shown that children as young as three years old start showing signs of discrimination against those that are different from them, and it is important to keep in mind that these are learned behaviors. No one is born with a prejudice; rather one is taught it or picks it up from the media and people he or she is exposed to.

As librarians, you're all fully aware of the life-changing power of books. The more stories you read and the more characters you interact with (though it's figurative), the more empathy you have for others. A great way to teach children about people other than them and those from their culture is with stories and books—and what better place to interact with stories and books than at the local public library? Now, here's where you step in. Is your collection diverse enough to accommodate for a global and diverse reader? Do you stand up for minorities and the discriminated-against by procuring and championing books by and about those people? Do you scan your books for hateful language?

There are many great tools and organizations out there to assist with the diversification of your collections. The trend #WeNeedDiverseBooks, American Library Services to Children's Dia programs and the Center for Children's Books at the University of Wisconsin–Madison are all great resources and good points of entry for tackling this beast of a problem. Let's say that your collection is as full and varied as the germs housed on our public computer's keyboards. Are your displays reflecting many different peoples and their stories? One way to incorporate a healthy variety of books into your displays is to intermingle books of other languages, or simply incorporating writings in other languages into the actual making of the display.

Speaking of implementing different languages, this is another great way to gain the family's trust during programming. The library that I currently have the pleasure of working at has me doing family story time on a regular basis, with crowds averaging at around 130 people. The community that I serve with this library is a rich and diverse one, with many families hailing from India, Pakistan, China, and Russia. I know this, not from making assumptions, but from talking with and listening to the children and their grown-ups during my day-to-day ventures around the department. Many of these families are new to America and the children are the first generation to be born here. The parents and guardians are eager to keep their children connected to their homeland, evidenced by their inquiry for books on and related to their countries as well as their use of their mother tongue with the children. A way for myself, a white native English-speaking Midwesterner, to connect with and acknowledge the differences among our patrons is to incorporate these variances into my programming.

Recently, I was doing a short literacy program for families where the topic was things that grow (fruit, vegetables, trees, towns, etc.). This program in particular was not at my home branch, so I was not familiar with any of the program's participants. With there only being about 30 in the room, I was able to have a longer and more detailed conversation with the children than the large family story time programs allow for. Thanks to children eager to tell their stories, the group—including myself—was able to learn a few words in Tamil as well as Spanish. The children swapped stories of their favorite fruits and vegetables and were surprised to learn that different families ate the foods in different ways (*we call it this and we eat it with this*, and *we call it that and we eat it with that*).

It is important to keep in mind that not all differences have to do with where on the Earth you're from. Those library buildings not in compliance with the American Disability Act are discriminating against and alienating groups of people who are handicapped. Children and families belonging to the LGBTQI+ community have been historically discriminated against in the library, as the majority of books banned in this country fall under the category of children's books and many have to do with the non-heteronormative content. Another people group to be mindful of is the homeless. The way in which the library interacts with all people groups has a large impact upon its youngest patrons. Children are very observant, even if they don't yet have the language to express themselves with. They notice that book covers are stereotypically pink and mild for girls and blue and action-packed for boys. They see the way the handicapped, homeless, and non-English speaking are dealt with, and it is making a mark on their young minds. If they observe adults speaking down to and belittling someone for being homeless, then that behavior is condoned and they very well may manifest it themselves. Imagine if we create places where empathy is shown in all interactions and people from all walks of life are welcome. What better way to invest in our future than to act now and lead by example? Incorporating diverse books, diverse languages, and diverse programs into your work will put you on the road toward cultural competence as well as foster an environment where all will feel welcome. But really, when we get down to the nitty-gritty, just be kind to one another and trust will follow.

The BIG Picture

No matter who your intended audience is, it is imperative to know them in order to best serve them. By actively listening to and meeting your patrons where they are (i.e., coming out from behind the desk), you can begin to gain an understanding of what your kids' needs and interests are, which will help you when creating programs for them.

Reflection Questions

1. On a scale of 1–10 (10 being the best), how would you rate your listening skills with children?
2. Are there any logistical and/or structural changes you can make to your space that will help to organize the chaos?
3. What rules can you establish in the children's/youth's department that will organize the chaos?

CHAPTER 4

Story Programming

So You've Got an Idea

When observing children during their free play, I am often surprised with how many of them create and direct their play with a story. *I'm the bad guy and I just chopped up all your underwear and now you've got to catch me!* When I was a child in elementary school, recess was dominated with stories of tornados coming to wreak havoc, causing my friends and me to run in the playground wildly looking for "shelter" and screaming manically, *There goes Mr. Smith's toupee! There goes Sarah's fake tooth!* Admittedly, we were not the coolest of the bunch, but that's beside the point. We had created a story and fully immersed ourselves in it. This is the same reason that the movie and TV industry dominates the entertainment world. In a relatively short period of time (90 minutes for a movie and 20–45 minutes for a TV episode) people can be absorbed into a story and transported out of their own life. Books are the same, though I'm only preaching to the choir when I say this.

All of the best games are heavily driven by a strong story; it's what draws us in. Everything, from video games to modern board games to interactive exhibits at museums, is carefully crafted by top-notch storytellers. The same way that stories in print and digital form (TV and movies) transport the readers/watchers, so too can a story-infused game or program. With the spy club, the overarching story of Ben Franklin's stolen cryptex is what hooked the children's interest and pulled them along week after week. The story grabbed their interest and allowed for their intrinsic motivation to be a part of the story to drive the boat.

In game design, there are two types of motivators: intrinsic and external. Intrinsic motivation comes from the belief that people are generally curious and apt to learning something new. Spinning educational lessons into a fun environment will allow for a natural expression of our innate curiosity to explore and absorb information. We'll discuss the educational bits of programming in Chapter 6, so for now let's focus on the story.

As librarians, or at the least library employees, you're surrounded by the best storytellers out there, so don't try and reinvent the wheel. Head to the stacks and see what's already a success. Picture books such as Graeme Base's *The Eleventh Hour* or the juvenile fiction *Escape from Mr. Lemoncello's Library* by Chris Grabenstein have opened up the door for a perfect marriage between games and stories. With these types of books, you could simply re-create the game illustrated in the novel, or simply take out bits and pieces of it.

The Eleventh Hour, for those of you unfamiliar with it, is the story of an elephant's 11th birthday party. Horace the Elephant works hard to prepare an entertaining shindig complete with a fabulous smorgasbord, but some sneaky guest steals all the food! It's up to the reader to track down and identify the thief. Everything, from the party invitations to the riddles provided throughout the book, could easily be replicated for a program. Simply take the story and reenact it in real life with a group of children. Similar programs could be offered with Grabenstein's book. Take the story and re-create it for children to live out. This type of copycat programming will work best with those kids who have not yet read the books. Otherwise, some ingenuity will be required of you to twist up and change the books' story so that the kids in the know will have some element of surprise, rather than blowing through the entire program and ruining the fun for everyone else.

Another great place to get ideas for your programming is to take a look at pop culture. What are kids these days interested in? The most direct way to enquire about current trends is to observe and interact with the kids you're trying to reach. Take note of what websites they visit while on the computers. Ask what games they have on their phones, what shows and movies they like to watch, and what activities they partake in at school. If they're elementary aged, then ask what they do during recess, or what they like to do for fun—outside of organized clubs and sport teams.

By casually interviewing children you will serve two purposes. First, you'll be gaining knowledge and insight into their worlds. This will help you better understand your audience and will, hopefully, give you some idea as to what programs you should offer. Second, your interest in the lives of these kids will speak volumes as it will communicate that you care for and are concerned about them. Doing some initial digging into the hot topics will help to increase your potential for success. It's incredibly frustrating to put so much of your time, blood, sweat, and tears into a program only to have no one show up. If you listen to the kids and offer something on par with their interests, then they will be more likely to participate. A great way to get a broad scope of your patrons' interests is to utilize passive surveys. The following is a sample survey that you can give to your young patrons to fill out while they wait for you to hunt down the last available copy of *Captain Underpants*.

Sample Survey for Passive Interviews

How old are you? _____

What's your favorite book/genre? _____

What's your favorite game (video or board game)? _____

What's your favorite movie? _____

What's your favorite TV show? _____

What do you like to learn about? _____

What do you want to be when you grow up? _____

As I mentioned earlier, another way to gather ideas for programming is to take a look at your circulation records. This is a good indication to what is currently trending and/or being taught on a large scale (i.e., the classroom). Speaking of the classroom, partnering with local schools and teachers is a great way to build a sense of community, show that you support the classroom, and help to expand the lessons being taught by the teachers. Let's say that the second graders at a local school are all working on a weather unit. They are studying the water cycle, natural disasters, and earth science in the classroom. By offering programs geared around what kids are already learning in the classroom, you can help teachers extend their influence, help students to expand upon their learning habits (get kids used to the idea that not all learning happens in the classroom), and help the library expand upon their patron participation.

Depending on what type of program you're planning to offer, your story will vary in detail and depth. If it's a passive program that is intended to be left out on tables over a weekend, then the story has to be quick to digest and able to stand on its own. Passive programs tend to be a crapshoot, as you don't know exactly who will show up or who will be there to help should assistance be required. I recently helped create a week-long passive program that was implemented in three different library buildings. The programs were to be left out during open hours, which covered several librarians' shifts on the reference desk. Some of the librarians were more inclined to help out and interact with children, while others were, well, less than enthusiastic. Case in point: One of the day's passive programs was a yoga station challenge. There were six silhouetted yoga poses printed out, laminated, and hung up in an open space near the reference desk. My shift that day didn't start until 5:00 p.m., and when I came in I was surprised to see that only six children had participated in the activity since 9:00 a.m. (tally marks were made on a sheet to quantify the daily programs). About 10 minutes into my time at the desk a six-year-old girl came up and inquired about the activity. After explaining that she had to try and mimic the yoga poses posted around the room, she was shy and didn't want to try. I promptly went out and began doing the challenge so that she wouldn't feel so alone and so she would have a model to follow. I went through each pose with her, and about 45 minutes and nearly 20 participants later I was finally able to make it back to the desk—but only after I went and pulled all of the yoga books we had so that the families involved could check them out. The yoga continued to be a hit for the remainder of the night, but it needed that initial push to get it started. As a passive program it was a success, yet it required a certain level of interaction from me. Had there not been a second person on the desk that evening, I wouldn't have been able to spend as much time as I did with the yoga. Had I not been limber and spry, I would not have been able to *do* the yoga.

When planning your programs, it is important to keep in mind the interest and ability levels of your fellow coworkers who will be involved in the implementation of your program—even if it's a passive one like the yoga was. Not everyone is gung ho about getting involved, and to each their own; however, things like this need to be taken into consideration. Another aspect of program planning to consider is that of your board and community. If you're going to offer a program that has the potential for controversy, then make sure that you are backed by your colleagues, boss, and board members.

If you're feeling lucky and want to try out a program without interviewing the kids, checking circulation trends, or reaching out to the schools, then more power to you! Not all ideas need to be fully fleshed out at the start. The very first idea I had for the spy club was specifically a STEM (science, technology, engineering, and math) and literacy-based program, where the kids would be given weekly STEM and literacy based missions. It wasn't until I sat down to plan and write that I got the "story" behind the idea. Other ideas are sometimes as simple as a theme (earth) or complex as a lesson plan (writing and creating books with a specific illustration technique). As cliché as it sounds, the most difficult part to running a marathon, or writing a program, is taking that first step. Once you get going, once you've got an idea, then the rest will follow. Let's say you've interviewed the kids, checked out what's trending, and talked with teachers or you jolted awake at 4:00 in the morning with a brilliant plan, and you've got your idea. Now what?

Goals

Similar to my writing process for picture books, I begin writing programs by going to the end and determining what the goals, or takeaways, are; then I go back and fill in the gaps to achieving said goals. When sitting down to write out your program, first ask yourself: What is it that you want your participants to walk away with? Do you want them to understand the way photosynthesis works? To be able to create their own circuit? To solve a mystery? If your program is purely for entertainment, then your goal would be something along the lines of "participant enjoyment" or "user engagement." No matter what the content of your program is, there is always a takeaway for you, your institution, and the patrons.

Start with your own goals. If goal setting is new to you, then I suggest you start with the big picture. Why are you doing this line of work? What inspires you? What do you want your legacy to be? I'm a big believer in having life goals. My goals help me to stay focused, and are what I turn to for motivation when feeling discouraged. When writing your own goals, try and keep them succinct. The format that I follow tends to be along the lines of the following:

I _____ (verb/work) for _____ (people/audience) because _____ (motivator).

Example: I write and illustrate picture books for young children because I believe in the transformative power of stories.

Example: I promote public libraries in the greater Chicagoland area because access to information and freedom of expression are paramount to democracy.

Bullet-style goals are also great, and are what I use when writing out daily goals. Once you've verbalized your BIG goal(s), then write it down and place it somewhere that you'll be able to see throughout the day—on your mirror, in your planner, on your desk, and so on.

Moving on to smaller goals; for your programs it's important to establish your own personal goals. Why are you creating this program? What do you hope to gain from it? Do you want to increase your circulation numbers of a specific topic? Do you want to get better at writing content? Perhaps it's not your goal at all; maybe your supervisor has charged you with the task of coming up with a new and exciting program. Whatever the case may be, try and get your own motivations down on paper so that at the end of the program you can go back and do a self-evaluation. When writing down your end goals, make them brief and simple. If a board member or supervisor comes and asks you why you should be allowed to create this program, you need to be able to quickly and concisely verbalize the goal, or purpose. A simple and well-worded end product will also be an easier target for you to aim toward, and when you know exactly what it is you're aiming for, that clarity will translate over into the creation process.

Next, think about what your institution's goals are with this program. Are they looking to get more foot traffic in the doors with a specific demographic or age range of people? Are they trying to change their reputation in the community? Again, for evaluation purposes it's good to get these things down in writing. These takeaways help to answer the *WHY.* When proposing an idea, especially one that's not been done before, it's vital to be able to answer the five Ws: who, what, where, when, and why. The who is your user group, the what is your idea, the where and the when are logistics, and the why is your goals.

The last goals that you want to get down on paper are those for the participants. What is it that you want *them* to take away from your program? If there is a specific classroom pillar that you're aiming to support, then write it down. If you want the kids to successfully work together as a team, then write it down. When evaluating each week's spy club meetings I went through a checklist that I had created that covered the STEM components as well as literacy and twenty-first-century skills. When creating each week's content, it was helpful to keep these quantifiers in mind when placing weekly goals and takeaways. See "Quantification and Assessment" in the Appendix for a detailed list of quantifiers.

Because the majority of my programming relies on stories, I like to think of myself as the writer and director of a play. As the director, I must know what happens at the beginning, middle, and end of the show to know how to direct the actors (kids, in our case). The very first thing I put down on paper when writing the spy club curriculum was the secret that was hidden in the cryptex at the end. The unveiling of that secret was the final act, the last hurrah before the curtain fell and the show was over. Once the secret was down, my closing act written, I go back and create the map that the children would follow to arrive there.

A Hook

Good stories, especially ones geared toward children, all begin with a hook. This hook is what initially grabs the attention of the reader/listener. A well-written program should have some sort of hook that will grab people's attention. Many libraries use their seasonal guides to promote programs, giving each event a short blurb or description. Those few sentences must be so well written that they engage the reader and bring them into the library, or at the very least make a phone call to inquire about more information. This may very well be the most difficult part of creating a program, for you're limited with your word count and must cram an entire program into a handful of carefully placed words. To help you with your blurb writing I suggest taking a look at advertisements geared toward young people. How do multimillion dollar companies appeal to kids? What is it that toy companies say in their commercials to get kids to beg their parents to purchase a game? Similarly, how do movie trailers compel people to go and drop their money in theaters? The ability to pitch a product is something that we will discuss in Chapter 7, when it comes to advertising, but these mechanics are also helpful in the planning process. Your hook needs to be rather simple and short, for many kids—especially those who aren't familiar with you and/or the library—won't give you much of their time. Your pitch has to be engaging, exciting, and able to capture their interest in a matter of minutes. Ever wonder why most successful movies for children begin with a traumatic event that leaves them parentless? This is because the trauma touches on the deepest fears of most children: to lose a parent; while simultaneously awakening one of their greatest desires: to be free, no rules, on their own. Viewers bond with the main character over their loss and cheer for their success as they venture out on their own to face the world. Voila! They're hooked!

Now, this is not to suggest that you traumatize your audience to gain their trust. Please, do NOT do that! There are other, less alarming ways to engage young minds. Think back to your own childhood; what was it that you were excited about? Odds are that kids today are excited by the same things. For some children, all you have to do is mention the name of their favorite game or movie and they're right there with you. The big-name corporations have already done the work of hooking their audience, and there's nothing wrong with piggybacking off of their success. In fact, if you are new to creating programs for children, then this would not be a bad way to get your feet wet.

Clubs are a current trend among the programs being offered to children, and the idea of a club is a hook in and of itself for many children. Several organizations have been hosting clubs for decades, and for them we are all extremely late to the game. Afterschool clubs, ranging in variety from chess to ping-pong, have long been popular in schools. Even in the world of libraries, clubs are far from new. However, what I am suggesting goes a bit beyond your standard book or movie club—not that those aren't great.

When kids create their own club, uninfluenced by adults, one of the first things that they do is create the qualifications for membership. *Boys only! 4th graders only!* This sense of exclusivity is a big draw for kids. For the spy club, membership was determined by an "official" application form. Spoiler alert—no one was rejected, but the kids didn't know that and so they felt that they belonged to an elite group (more on this in the next section) and that was enough to keep them coming back week after week. Clubs are by far my favorite type of program style, as they lend themselves so nicely to the age bracket that I primarily work with (elementary) and allow for loose structure as well as sanction my leadership role while still enabling me to be in on the fun.

Special events that only meet once can have just as great of an impact as the longer multiday/multiweek programs. As of my writing this in 2017, one of the hot trends among libraries is to host an Escape Room. These programs involve "locking" a group of people in a room and giving them the goal of solving a series of riddles/puzzles to uncover the key and "escape" in a given amount of time. Since these rooms are a popular experience outside of the library (and people are willing to pay $30/person), the hook is already taken care of and we're just riding on their coattails (the *free* aspect of library programs doesn't hurt either). There are several types of programs you can offer to your patrons, depending on what will work for your library, a few of which are as follows:

- Author/Illustrator visit
- Public figure visit
- Meet and greets
- Readings
- Art club
- Book club
- Coding club
- Drag queen story time
- Origami club
- Science club
- Spy club
- Escape room
- Game nights
- Game tournaments

- Showcases
- Master classes
- Writing groups
- Reading programs
- Oral storytellers
- Plays
- Film festivals

When it comes to selecting the type of program you want to offer, the sky is the limit. Let your creativity fly, and who knows? Perhaps you'll think up the next hot programming trend! Once you've determined who your intended audience is, what your goals are, and what type of program you want to offer, then it's time to start setting the scene.

Setting the Scene

The dreaded line "We've never done it that way before" has been used as a roadblock, an obstruction of the most infuriating kind, for several programs I've pitched over the years. My initial instinct is to scream, "SO WHAT?" But I do NOT do that, because I'm trying very hard to be an adult. Instead, when creating a program I try to set the scene in a way that makes it irresistible for people to turn down. Obviously, it hasn't always worked.

When I say "setting the scene," I'm not speaking of the decorations or actual setup of the program. I'm referring to the setup of the idea of the program. For the spy club, this included the initial pitch and overarching storyline, which went something like this:

> Back when our Founding Fathers still roamed the streets of Philadelphia, before there were video games and cell phones, Ben Franklin was searching for a place to hide something. Something so secret and momentous that he decided to hide it in a cryptex and entrusted it in the care of the city's most elite information agents: the librarians at the Free Library of Philadelphia. These librarians were the first agents in the Free Library of Philadelphia Espionage Agency (FLPEA) and have been protecting Mr. Franklin's secret for decades.
>
> Recently, there was a breach of security and the cryptex was stolen! Due to the nature of the crime, the authorities have reason to believe that it was an inside job: a rogue agent/librarian. Because of the sensitivity of the contents, the FLPEA has decided to keep the robbery from the public's knowledge and handle the investigation internally, with a new recruit of agents.

The scene is set, and by the time I had finished giving this pitch to the powers that be, not only were they hooked and supportive of this project, but they doubled my funding right there on the spot. Granted, my initial budget was only $250, bringing my new total to $500, nevertheless I had set the scene and gotten my benefactors excited about what was to come—imagine how excited the kids were when they found out that they were to be the new recruits!

There are two steps when setting the scene. First is the writing. Second is the pitching. When writing the scene, it helps to have a good understanding of how stories work. We briefly went over the *hook* aspect of storytelling in the previous section, so now we're getting on to the meatier bits of fleshing out the idea. This step is all about capturing the imagination of your audience. What this is doing is bringing a story to life, and it's what is going to set your program apart from all the others. People want to be a part of an epic story. That's why they read books, go to movies, and watch TV. What you can offer your patrons with this type of programming is an invitation to take part in a living and breathing story. The kids at my library branch were intrigued with the idea of being a spy, yet when I offered them books based on the topic they weren't interested. However, when I invited them to actually *be* spies and step into the world of the FLPEA, they took to it like fish to water. You don't have to be a prolific author to come up with a compelling scene; you just need to be observant. This is where it is helpful to interview your prospective audience and get an insight into what books and hobbies they're interested in.

There are typically three parts to a complete story: the beginning, the middle, and the end. The beginning is your hook/pitch, the end is your takeaway/final goal(s), and the middle is where your audience will fill in the gaps. The question you must ask yourself at this point in the creation process is *how do participants fit into the storyline?* When setting the scene you're giving a rundown of the program, while simultaneously inviting patrons to participate. You're *hooking* them and *reeling them in.* With the FLPEA, I hooked the kids by telling them about the robbery, and then invited them to participate by offering them applications to join the hunt as FLPEA agents.

By creating a spot for your patrons to fill, you're inviting them to a party where there's already a place set for them at the table. I've witnessed children and teens pass up on programs simply because they felt that it "wasn't for them," for reasons ranging in scope from not being intrigued by what was being offered to not having a buddy to participate with. By offering a program that is reliant on participants, rather than the information (or on you as the leader), these kids feel a sense of purpose in joining and will be more likely to return for future events.

Bear with me for a moment while we briefly dive into the world of inquiry-based learning, for this is at the heart of revolving programs around the participant, opposed to the content. As librarians, we are not the main educators of children and youth. Teachers are the ones trained for creating lesson plans and preparing their students for academic success; we're merely an extension and support of that classroom activity (or living room, including homeschoolers). Since librarians aren't responsible for the heavy-duty lifting when it comes to education, we are free to utilize a variety of teaching techniques paired with a variety of topics, inquiry-based learning being one.

In order to explain what inquiry-based learning is, let's imagine a classroom. The students are all seated at desks, while the teacher is in the front dispersing information. Students are expected to memorize and regurgitate said information via tests, which are then assessed for competency in a very binary way (you're either right or wrong). In the inquiry-based classroom, the teacher is not at the front spewing out information; rather he or she is among the students occasionally giving information, but more often encouraging students to dig for information on their own based on their curiosity about the subject matter.

For instance, the topic for the day could be the earth's layers. With a brief introduction to what comprises the layers of our planet, students are then encouraged to talk among themselves and dig deeper for information related to this topic, letting their curiosity drive the boat. One student may look up how scientists extract ice samples with long pipes down in Antarctica, while another may explore volcanoes. This style of learning takes the emphasis away from the teacher as "informant" and changes his or her role to "facilitator," while giving the reins to the students. We'll get into more of this inquiry-based learning in Chapter 6, but for this chapter, all we need to keep in mind is that this student-focused learning style will help to give participants a sense of purpose in the program—not to mention it will give them a break from the traditional way of learning.

As I mentioned earlier, an overly complicated storyline is not needed for a program to be successful. All you really have to do is hook the children's and youth's attention and give them an "in" into the program. Even if you're hosting a video game tournament, by hooking them with popular games that they're already playing at home, you can "reel them in" by having a spot for them to fill in the bracket. Taking this in another direction, when doing story time with the younger kids and their families, you can hook them with a theme that interests them (the most recent one I did was all about BUGS) and reel them in by making it an interactive experience. The scene that my current library sets for our all-ages story time is one filled with music, dancing, read-alouds, and puppets. Crowds of over 100 show up for these story times because they know that they will be interesting and that they're welcome/wanted.

Oftentimes setting the scene is very much reliant on your own personal interactions with patrons. It comes down to how users perceive you, not how you perceive yourself. Even if you think you're the most open and approachable person in your department, if a patron thinks otherwise, then there's a problem. The scene that you set on a daily basis in your department will speak volumes to the programs that you offer. If you're not inclined to play with the kids, then why would they want to participate in a maker program with you? Consistency in your attitude toward patrons from the reference desk to the program room will build your reputation up as approachable and will allow for you to gain the trust of children, teens, and their families.

Once your hook and invitation are written, when the scene is set, then it's time for you to burn it into your mind. Odds are, after spending a good chunk of time writing out these two things, the concept you're going for is already ingrained into your brain. Knowing your story is vital when pitching it to fellow library employees, board members, and—most importantly—the children and youth. If you're hesitant on a detail or aspect of the story/program, then people will pick up on that and it will take away the legitimacy of your creation. You must immerse yourself in the story, so that you can answer any and all questions about the program as well as add to the magic of creating this new and exciting learning environment.

Weeks before I kicked off the official FLPEA spy club, I had already convinced my kids that I was a secret agent for the library. I had so immersed myself into the story of Ben Franklin and his cryptex that I was able to act it out with ease and confidence. This attitude was noted by the kids and gave an air of magic to the entire program. Because I was so convinced of the story, the kids (and some adults) were able to buy into it quickly and with abandon. We were all in on it together, and though I was the one in charge, I knew no more details than what was sent over from headquarters each week in the mission assignments. If one mission dealt with the different states of water (solid, liquid, and gas), then I was merely there to point them in the direction of information resources that they could use to further explore the topics. Inquiry was king; it led the agents down many exciting and new paths.

The BIG Picture

Story-driven programs are a powerful way to engage young minds with information and knowledge. To maximize your chances for success, make sure you're offering programs that are of interest to your intended audience. Clearly define the goals for yourself, your institution, and your participants. This will help with planning as well as evaluation after the program is completed.

Reflection Questions

1. How well do you know your audience? Write down at least five topics you believe to be popular with your indented age group.
2. What is your BIG Picture goal for working in libraries?
3. What are some unique ways you can "sell" a program to your patrons?

CHAPTER 5

Planning Your Program

How to Build a Time Frame for Your Program

Time. There's never enough of it unless of course you've designed a program with not enough content, and you've got 30 six- and seven-year-olds expectantly staring at you with 45 minutes left in the program and nothing to do. Then, the seconds drag on as time comes dangerously close to a full and complete stop. We're going to focus on time management for programming in three separate areas. First, the time needed for creation (writing) of the program. Second, the time needed for marketing and setup of the program. Third, and final, the time needed for the implementation of the program.

If you've got a good sense of your own work pace, then you will be able to give yourself concrete and realistic time frames for all three areas that need management. For instance, I know that I am relatively quick at writing content for programs, but I dramatically slow down when it comes to marketing and the actual setup of each event. If you're collaborating with other people on creating an event, then stating each of your strengths and weaknesses can help to determine job duties. If someone is an excellent writer, then perhaps he or she can be the one designated to take minutes during your meetings and type up the actual content. If someone else is better at coming up with zany and fun ideas, but in a more abstract way, then having another person in place to write down these ideas will take the pressure off of him or her to do so, freeing him or her up to shout out ideas as they flow into his or her train of thought.

If you're not collaborating with others, then I would always err on the side of caution and allow yourself extra time to pull off your program in its entirety. Once you become versed in content creation, implementation, and quantification, you'll be able to work at a faster pace in addition to having a stockpile of ideas to draw upon for last-minute needs. Let's be practical for a minute though and acknowledge the fact that time is sparse and devoting large amounts to programming isn't always feasible. From cataloging to weeding, to making sure the tables and chairs aren't covered in mysterious materials, programming often gets put on the back burner, and understandably so. A dilemma to say the least, but one that we can navigate around.

The first time that you walk yourself through the program-creation process that I have outlined in this book may take you a considerable amount of time, as you familiarize yourself with the theory behind this way of programming as well as the jargon that goes with it. Fear not! The first time is the hardest, and—I promise—the more content you create, the easier this will become. Your thought process will morph over time, allowing you to verbalize goals, hooks, teaching points, and so on with ease and speed.

Included in the creation phase of planning is a good amount of time that should be devoted to research of the topic at hand. Educate yourself on the topic at hand, or, at the very least, know what resources there are available for the patrons to do their own searching in. But I highly recommend learning the content yourself. Even if you're just hosting a movie night, watch the movie—in entirety—beforehand. There could be a great opportunity for a teachable moment based on what's in the film, and being prepared will make it all the more impactful. If you're hosting an event where the kids will be making something, then make it yourself ahead of time. Do what it is you're asking your participants to do. In testing it all beforehand, you'll work out the kinks and, hopefully, learn something new along the way. The more confident you are with the material, the easier it will be to teach and the more at ease your audience will be.

Now, even if you do your own research ahead of time and prepare yourself mentally for the program, I can almost guarantee that there will be a time when a child or teen asks a question that you don't know the answer to. This is a great opportunity to show that even adults are still learning, as well as show off the trove of resources at your location. Pretending to know it all sends a misleading message, because you don't. No one does. Showing humility in this type of scenario and admitting that you need to do some research to find out will set an example of lifelong learning habits and curiosity for the youths and, believe me, they will take note.

One of the reasons that I work in informal education settings, opposed to the classroom, is because I am a fervent believer in lifelong learning. The majority of what I have learned thus far in life has come to me outside of the classroom. I was lucky enough to have adults in my life to model this attitude of perpetual learning, and it made a big impact on my life. Children and teens today, especially the ones who don't do well in the current education system, need to see that there is more learning than what is taught with textbooks and exams. Modeling curiosity about the world at large may very well be one of the biggest impacts you can have on a student. So crack open those books, use the databases, and let the kids see that you too are still a student at heart.

Depending on what type of program you have in mind, your time frame will vary in accordance with the amount of research and writing to be done. For myself, I plan on at least 1 hour of prep time for every 30 minutes of program time (i.e., if it's a one-hour program, then I plan on two hours for researching and writing). Some of you will need more time, while others need less. Whatever the case may be, just make sure to devote enough time for the prep work, so as to be fully prepared and to work out as many rough spots as possible.

If you're wanting to create a club-based program, similar to what I did with the spy club, then you'll need to set aside a sizable chunk of time to create the entire curriculum before the club even starts. After I determined what the goals were, wrote the hook, and decided on doing a club style program that would meet once a week for 14 weeks, I sat down and wrote all 14 weeks of the spy club material over the course of 2 weeks.

When writing multimeeting events, you should have a notebook handy as well as a calendar with your own personal events as well as your institution's calendar of events. If you know that the third week in May is going to be absolute mayhem with summer reading right around the corner, then plan on having a light week as far as prep and setup go for your program. Don't burn yourself out, for it will not only have ramifications for you but the quality of programming will begin to fade along with your energy levels and enthusiasm. Choose a time frame that is feasible for you, as well as for the amount of material that you have to offer. The last thing you want is to drag a program on for six weeks when it really should have only gone on for two. Be smart with your time and resources and plan accordingly.

As I mentioned, I wrote a 14-week program for the spy club that met once a week for the pilot program. After its success, I was asked to rewrite the program for a club that met 5 days a week for 12 weeks. Since the goals, hook, and invitation remained the same, all I had to do was follow the lesson templates I had previously created and come up with enough content to fill in the additional eight hours for each week. This was much easier said than done, but it was not impossible. By this point, I was well aware of my own strengths, and knew that I would need several weeks to write out the content. Because I was so well versed with the concept of the spy club and the story that went with it, I was able to elaborate on the missions/activities and storyline with relative ease. Had I been writing the entire summer program from scratch, it would have been quite a difficult undertaking indeed.

Marketing. Oh, boy. This is not my favorite aspect of the job; nevertheless, it is very important. The good news is that your creativity is just as welcome here as it is in the writing process. I didn't have time to make fliers and web pages to market the spy club, so I went down a rabbit hole that I wasn't initially sure I would get out of. I decided to let the kids do all the marketing for me; only I used reverse psychology and swore them to secrecy. In the application to become a Free Library of Philadelphia Espionage Agency (FLPEA) agent, there is a secrecy clause that all must sign. It states that "Above all else, I [. . .] promise to keep the FLPEA and all the missions I'm sent on, TOP SECRET." On the very first day of the club, I had 10 applicants. The next week I had 16 followed by 20, culminating at the end of the program with over 50 enrolled agents. We'll get into more of the specifics with marketing in Chapter 7, but be sure to leave plenty of time in place for this aspect of creating a buzz around what you're offering at your library.

Setting up for your program, should it involve a lot of props and/or pieces, should be done as early as possible. Always allow for extra time, in case you've forgotten something, or leaving room for troubleshooting should something go squirrelly. The rule of thumb that I follow for program setup is a minimum of 30 minutes followed by a 30-minute teardown after the program is over. It's important to remember that more doesn't always mean *better*. Your story and overall ambiance that you set will engage these kids and teens more than decorations and/or props will. If it takes you longer to do the physical setup than it did the writing of the program, then you may want to reevaluate your goals and content.

The most time-consuming aspect in creating this learning playground that we're striving for is in the actual, physical setting up of the event. In my mind I can set up a construction exercise in a matter of minutes, but in reality it takes me closer to a solid 20 minutes to get everything laid out and ready, complete with an example. Part of the way that I incorporate inquiry-based learning into my programs is by having an elementary example of the day's task set out for observation. Many of my passive programs revolve around that train of thought. I set out the activity, make a basic example, and then let the kids have a go at it. I don't want to lecture them; they just got out of school where they've been talked at for hours, and I don't want to give away the entire lesson either, hence the very basic example. I just want to whet their appetite and let their own curiosity and imagination lead the way. More on this, as well as maker spaces, in the next chapter.

Implementation is the fun part, and—so long as you're prepared—the time will fly by; it always does when you're having fun. Setting a time limit on your daily events will give you a parameter to work in, not to mention the fact that it will give you a definite time to say, "okay, time to go home now!" My spy club meetings were two hours long, not a minute more nor less. The agents knew the drill, and would anxiously stare at the clock willing the hands to strike 4:00 p.m. so they could get on with their mission. They also knew that when those same hands struck 6:00 p.m., the meeting was over and it was time for them to leave and begin looking forward to the next week's meeting. With a 4:00 p.m. start time, it gave me 30 minutes to set up and 15 minutes to tear down after the kids left at 6:00 p.m. Although the length of time it took the kids to complete a task varied with the amount that showed up for any given meeting, I knew more or less that a two-hour window allowed for one training exercise and two missions. Even on days when it was just me and 30 agents ranging in age from 3 to 16 years old, we were able to stick to the time frame. Had I limited my meeting to only third through fifth graders, then I would probably have been able to squeeze in more content, or at least made the two missions more complex. But seeing as it was an open program that didn't require advanced registration and was welcoming of all ages, I had to keep to my aforementioned plan of action.

If you're unsure of how long it will take your participants to complete a task, then err on the side of caution and overplan. It is far better to have things that you weren't able to get to rather than coming up short and having a group of kids or teens staring at you expectantly while you sweat and rack your brain for jokes or riddles to distract them from the fact that you've got dead air. I speak from experience, and let me tell you, the kids were not impressed with my jokes nor did they leave with an overwhelming desire to return. Pro-tip: Have a good joke book, game, or activity on backup for you never know when you'll need it!

Writing Weekly/Daily Lesson Plans

If we're looking at your program from a bird's eye view, then we should be able to see the big picture: who the program is for, what it's about, and how you'll hook and reel participants in, as well as what type of program it is and what the duration will be. Now, we're going to zoom in and look at the content from a more granular perspective. Writing out program plans is not difficult, especially if you've got the aforementioned nailed down. These program plans will serve to give you a point of reference during the actual event as well as to help you quantify throughout and afterward.

Each program plan should start with a brief introduction of yourself as well as of the program. *Welcome to Spy Club, I'm Special Agent Rose . . .* Or, *Welcome to Family Story Time! My name is Miss Brittany . . .* If this is a singular program, or the first day of a multiday program, then it bears repeating the hook. This will engage students again, getting them excited for what's to come.

There are many ways to write out program plans, with each catering to a different type of person/presenter, but we're going to stick to two different formats. The first format is in depth and serves as a type of script to follow. The second type is skeletal, or an outline, with bullets of the pertinent information. If you're not sure what type of presenter you are, then I suggest starting out with the in-depth program plan and weening yourself down to the bulleted version over time. Or, you very well may prefer to stick with the detailed script permanently, as it fits your style best. I know many classroom teachers who, after years of teaching, still write out and follow VERY detailed lesson plans, and all the more power to them!

In-Depth Program Planning

One of the greatest benefits of the in-depth program planning is that it allows for anyone to pick up the paperwork and be able to pull off the program, whereas the skeletal plan requires some insight into the preparation and planning of the curriculum. With in-depth programming, if you were to become violently ill just hours before your big event, the substitute librarian would (should) be able to pick up your program plans, follow them verbatim, and successfully host your event.

In-depth program planning also tends to give you a minute-by-minute breakdown of your event, helping you to stick to the intended time frame. Back when I was teaching at a zoo, I used in-depth program plans because I had 30 six-year-olds for six hours, five days a week. It was much too in-depth for me to possibly have memorized all, or even a portion of the content, so I relied heavily on my plans. There is a certain amount of stress that comes with the task of not only keeping 30 six-year-olds alive, well and out of the tiger's habitat, but of actually imparting biology and animal science knowledge to them in an age-appropriate and exciting manner. This stress was very much ameliorated by having such a solid and deep program plan to lean on. If your program has the potential to be a handful, then having this type of guide will serve you well.

For example, if you're doing a program for a group of second graders about herbivores, and you want to talk about how scientists can differentiate between the different types of animals based on their diet, then you can talk about teeth. Most second graders have lost a tooth, or are well on their way to losing their first (and will be more than enthusiastic about showing you their gut-wrenching tooth that can wiggle and swing in the breeze as it clings to its last string of gum). Herbivores have flat teeth, used for grinding plants, while carnivores have sharp and jagged teeth, used for ripping flesh and meat. Having the kids use their tongues to feel their own teeth or look into their neighbor's mouths to observe their teeth will reveal that we have both flat and sharp teeth. This means that we are designed to eat both plants and animals, and the word for that is OMNIVORE!

By writing out an in-depth lesson plan (see In-Depth Lesson Information in the Appendix), you can go into your programs confident that you've got enough information and material to fill the entire program. If you're able to "translate" information into an age-appropriate manner on the spot, then feel free to write in a way that feels natural to you. If that makes you nervous, then write the lesson information in vocabulary that is appropriate for the intended audience. Another component to being age appropriate is using language that the audience is familiar with. If the group doesn't understand what the words that are coming out of our mouth mean, then—*surprise*—you are not communicating successfully. This isn't to say that you must only use words that your audience knows. On the contrary, you can make them "reach up" and learn new vocabulary, either by inferring meaning from the context or by point blank explaining the meaning.

Skeletal Program Planning

Inquiry-based programs lend themselves to skeletal program planning, as you merely serve as a guide to information rather than *the* informant. Most skeletal programs can fit on to one or, maybe, two pages. The idea behind this plan, or guide, is to give you a minimalist style road map of your program presentation. You've got general ideas down, with perhaps a few extra details, but the majority of the information retrieval will be left up to the participants and their own digging into information.

Bullet-formatted program planning is not a shortcut for in-depth planning, nor is it any easier. When you're writing down only the main thoughts/actions to implement, then you have to be so comfortable with the

> **FLPEA: Andorra Branch Case #008**
>
> **Materials Provided by Headquarters:**
> - SOMA Cube
> - Seeds
>
> **Action:** Seeds
>
> **Mission:**
>   Step One: We at the FLPEA Headquarters have been sent highly sensitive information regarding the Global Seed Vault. On Svalbard, a small island owned by Norway in the Arctic Circle, lies the key to humankind's survival on Earth: the Global Seed Vault. A sample of every single kind of seed known to man is kept deep in the side of a mountain at the GSV. If ever there were to be a cataclysmic disaster on our planet, this seed vault would be able to restore Earth's crops thus providing food for humans and animals to survive once more. GSV has sent over a map of their seed deposits, but due to the sensitive nature of the mission it's been taken apart and put on a SOMA Cube. Step one of your mission is to work together as a team to construct the cube, and piece the map together.
>   Step Two: The GSV has recently had it's first withdrawal from Syria due to the war currently going on. While the Syrians were in the mountain receiving their wheat seeds someone disguised as a Norwegian GSV guard managed to make a withdrawal without the proper paperwork. On the way out, this mystery person dropped some of the seeds they had taken. We at headquarters have narrowed the unknown seeds down to six possible variations. It's up to you to analyze the seeds and determine what kind it is. Once you have determined what kind of seed was picked up, then place it on the Global Seed Vault map. The native land of the seed may be where our thief is headed!
>
> **Notes on Seed:**
> _____
> _____
> _____
> _____
> _____
>
>   Signature: _____

Figure 5.1: Example of a weekly mission plan

material on hand that you can easily create "filler" or talk at random on the subject with authority. You must also be able to anticipate the various directions that your program could go and be prepared mentally to address all inquiries. This isn't to scare you away from creating this kind of master plan, but to serve as a gentle reminder that when you're striving for quality programming, you must be willing to put in the work and become a quality presenter of information.

I digress. Here is an example of a weekly mission plan for the spy club. This type of program planning makes the actual, physical plans part of the program itself while also placing me on par with the students. I was not teaching down to them, but rather giving them a brief introduction to the week's mission. There even came a point in the club when a few agents became confident enough in their reading skills that they offered to read the week's mission to the group. I had inadvertently given away my job, and was left with minor crowd control tasks. This was a miracle in and of itself, considering when I first started working with this group of kids they were so unsure of their reading abilities that they refused to read aloud to me, hated working on their reading assignments, and wouldn't be caught dead checking out a book to read at home. Now, here they were standing in front of their peers reading with confidence and gusto! I immediately began to increase the level and complexity of vocabulary into the mission statements as a way to help them with their literacy skills. Words that they did not know were sounded out, and even given to the group to look over together to decipher.

People are naturally curious creatures, and when given the opportunity for exploration, you are opening up a world of possibilities. This is great, but you must be able and willing to go down the various roads with your participants. If, when hosting a game night, rather than having your kids or teens play established games, you encourage them to make and play their own, then you must be willing and prepared to discuss a cornucopias of things such as game mechanics, creativity, player management, and math concepts, just to name a few. If you cannot create a bulleted outline of this type of program and rely on your own knowledge to fill in the gaps or direct participants to reliable sources, then you either need to school yourself a bit more on the topic at hand or get your resource ducks in a neat and tidy line so that they are ready for action the moment you call upon them.

Regardless of whether you write an in-depth or skeletal program plan, or if you don't write one at all, there are some key things to remember in imparting knowledge to kids and teens. To be able to connect information of any kind to real-life scenarios will help to reinforce the concepts being taught. You can tell a child that a whale shark is about 41 feet from snout to tail and leave it at that. This measurement is an abstract concept, and for younger audiences it will not serve as a concrete image. Now, if you were to go on and say that the whale shark is about the same size as a yellow school bus, just like the ones that they'll ride home in that day, then you've connected information to their everyday life and made the abstract concrete. For many students, images of whale sharks will float through their minds every time they see a school bus from then on out. For many of them this will not be the case, but my point is that when you are able to make connections between familiar objects or ideas and abstract theories or information, then you greatly increase the potential for retention.

Coming Up with Supporting Activities to Reinforce Concepts Being Taught

It was 3:45 p.m. on a Tuesday evening, our spy club day, and the air started to buzz with excitement and anticipation for the week's meeting. Five minutes later, the agents began lining up at the doors that lead to the basement where our meetings were held, safe from the prying eyes of *other* spies and nonagents. At exactly 4:00 p.m., I led the group of positively giddy agents down the stairs and to their training exercise: a minefield. Much to my surprise, the kids were well aware of what a minefield was and how it operated, a sign of the times I suppose. I had created a minefield simulation course using only black squares of construction paper taped down to the floor in a 6 × 12 grid. There are about a hundred variations of this game that you can use, all with varying time and financial commitments tied to them. Seeing that I was strapped on time and was pinching my pennies, I went with supplies that I had at my disposal. I had printed out "keys," which showed the same grid with 72 squares (6 × 12) and had used a marker to X out my "hidden mines." Each agent "planted" a total of 10 mines on his or her own key sheets, and then turned them in to me. The first agent in line was the first "commander" selecting a key from the pile and calling out directives to the agent attempting to cross the field. *Move one square to your right, then one square forward! No! No! Not that one!* Upon activating a hidden mine, the commander would either make an explosive sound with his or her mouth (we had some *very* talented sound artists) or call out a body part that was just lost; *There goes your left leg! Off went your butt!* Even top secret agents still enjoy a good butt reference.

This training exercise was such a huge hit that I opened it back up after the missions were complete, something that headquarters usually didn't allow. The agents had a blast, were actively engaged in sharpening their literacy skills by calling out verbal cues (not to mention the skill required to come up with more and more unique and hilarious outcomes for activating a mine), utilized resource management when it was their turn to create the field, and were given only a certain number of "bombs," as well as touching on a handful of twenty-first-century skills, and this was all done for the grand price of $0. I could have gone to a lot more detail in presenting this game, by buying plastic cups and "activating" mines by placing confetti or glitter under specific ones so that when they're stomped on, a grand and sparkly mess is made, indicating a mine went off. This wouldn't have depleted my funds, and it may have even been a better visual than what I offered, but it would have taken much more time to set up in-between rounds in addition to causing a mess of the most massive and frustrating sort (due to the magical staying powers of glitter).

Being able to host a program under a tight or nonexistent budget is a skill that I know many librarians intuitively have. The ability to stretch a penny while maintaining quality and class is a valuable skill to have and will open up the doors to infinite possibilities. As I mentioned in the prelude, I was able to create a "high-tech spy phone" using just a piece of lined notebook paper and a little bit of acting (Oscar-worthy if I do say so myself). The minefield was a success because I sold it as a sanctioned training exercise from headquarters, which gave it legitimacy and an air of adventure, two key elements to a successful program. Good program development and putting your heart into an activity can make up for a lack of funds; however, a boatload of money could never make up for a lack of heart or good program development. If you think what you're offering is fun, then the kids will pick up on that and be more inclined to enjoy it themselves.

When coming up with activities to support the concepts you're trying to teach, it's helpful to know what resources you have at your disposal. Don't underestimate the power that a skein of yarn or a clear plastic tube can have. Take stock of EVERYTHING so that when it comes to creating events, you'll have a stockpile of items to draw upon for creative and innovative ways to implement lessons. If you've got storage space, then asking for donations of items that have some life left in them (I accept anything but clothing, for reasons relating to things that crawl) is a great way to build up your reserve of supplies. Old bikes, computers, toys, kitchen gadgets, games, and the list goes on and on as does the limit to what you could do with such items.

A popular trend that has been taking place in library programs is a take-apart club, where students (usually elementary aged) are invited to come and literally take apart things ranging from toys to small appliances. This type of activity is reliant on either donations or someone with a knack for surfing garage sales for good deals. Kids are given lessons in how to use tools and then encouraged to dissect their object piece by piece in order to better understand the components used as well as the reasoning behind them. Some of my favorite books in the nonfiction collection are the ones based on how things work, which go hand in hand with a program such as this. Low cost, high return; that's what this style of programming is all about.

When planning for a program based on the Earth's layers, I read through some of the nonfiction picture books of the same topic and came across a page that talked about how scientists in Antarctica would hammer large pipes down into the ice and pull up a sample to observe and analyze the layers. One section of ice brought up with the pipe revealed a multitude of layers, indicating different years/decades that the ice had been there. With this factoid in mind, I took some Mason jars that had been lying around, bought four different flavored/colored Jell-O packages for a buck a piece, and made my own "layers dig" experiment for a biweekly homeschooler program I helped host at the library.

I prepared all five Jell-O solutions in five separate bowls using a turkey baster filled in the first layer. I varied the kinds and amount of Jell-O used in each jar, so that when I was complete, no jar's layers would be the same. After refrigerating the first layer for 30 minutes, I repeated with the second layer, refrigerated, third layer, refrigerated, and so on. When completed, the jars each had 10 layers of varying colors, textures, and thicknesses. While rummaging through the baking drawer at home, I had come across some dinosaur sprinkles and embedded them into a few of the Jell-O layers for texture and to simulate embedded fossils. Seeing that the jars were clear, and would immediately reveal the number and color of the layers, I wrapped the outside of them with aluminum foil. Then I took some leftover pliable and clear plastic tubing (about 0.75 inch in diameter) that was used for the heat/vac system, cut it into six-inch sections, and instructed the kids to slowly press them into the samples. By placing a hand over the open end of the tube to create suction, they were able to pull the tube and Jell-O sample out of the jar. The various layers came out in the tubes and the kids wrote down how many layers they counted, what color they were, and whether or not they had any texture. We were able to make the connection between what the kids were doing with the Jell-O and what scientists do with ice, and had some great discussions about how it was tricky to pull out all of the layers of Jell-O and how much more difficult it must be with massive pipes and hard ice. This was a fun activity for the Earth's layers program that cost under $5 to create, allowed for a real-world connection, and stemmed from reading an article in a nonfiction picture book.

From teaching physics via "Ghostly Bowling" with an $0.89 pumpkin and some recycled cereal boxes painted white with faces drawn on (to look like ghosts) to talking about aerodynamics with paper planes, the examples of cheap yet successful activities are 10-fold, and I've only just scratched the surface. From the seemingly bottomless pit that is Pinterest to the American Library Association's programming boards, there are many resources available for coming up with creative ways to teach kids about anything under the sun. Your fellow employees and patrons (especially parents) are another great resource to go to when coming up with innovative ideas. Many people have explored the four corners of the earth with their children without ever leaving their own backyards or breaking the bank. Perhaps you won't be able to recreate the jerry-rigged rocket launch that a patron did with his five-year-old, but it may spark a new idea in you that might be wildly successful with your fifth graders. Inspiration is a funny thing, as you never quite know when it will strike, but odds are the more people you communicate with and the more you experiment yourself, the greater your capacity for innovative thinking will be.

The BIG Picture

We are all unique individuals and the way in which we write and prepare our plans will be as varied as the programs we offer. Whether you write your lesson plans in great detail, in bullet point thoughts, or a combination of the two, having some sort of preplanned and organized thought process will help to bring a level of confidence and organization to your program.

Reflection Questions

1. Whether you're planning a birthday party, a drop-in program, or a massive event for the library, how do you prepare? Days in advance? Last minute? Collaborate with others?

2. As far as program planning goes, where do you fall on the prep spectrum below?

    In-depth writing   Heaving bullets   Bullet thoughts   Skeletal   No prep

3. What resources are at your disposal for coming up with supporting activities for your programs? Pinterest? An innovative patron or staff member? Partnerships with local museums?

CHAPTER 6

Full STEAM Ahead!

What Is STEAM?

Aside from F-R-E-E, the hottest four letters in children's programming today are STEM (science, technology, engineering, and math). Occasionally, an "A" gets thrown in the mix (STEAM) to incorporate the arts, but what are emphasized are the four core disciplines. This acronym wasn't made popular until the early 2000s, but the idea behind STEM/STEAM isn't new. Interdisciplinary curriculum, or the connecting of more than one discipline in a single lesson, has been around for ages, and it's a concept that is effective and makes sense for preparing students for interactions within the world at large.

The compartmentalization of the school day is disjointed and doesn't properly reflect the way that they will be required to think and carry out duties as a functioning adult. Math for 30 minutes, followed by science for 30 minutes, followed by physical education for 30 minutes, and so on is not the way that the world outside of the classroom works. As adults, we don't have the luxury of compartmentalizing our daily tasks, whether we're in the workplace, at a social event, or at home. It's all interconnected and is related to one another.

While there are many hurdles that classroom teachers face when attempting to incorporate interdisciplinary curriculums, we as librarians don't have to worry about such things and are free to make all of the connections we can fit into our allotted time slot. Teaching students to be able to connect disciplines within one experience will help them have a wider angle with which they view the world, and will serve them well as they maneuver through life. There's nothing quite as thrilling for me, as an educator, as when I'm able to observe students making those connections between disciplines themselves.

During week two of the spy club, headquarters sent over ice samples (golf ball–sized ice spheres) that an agent on the field in Antarctica had collected and shipped to Philadelphia for analysis. The ice samples came from Deception Island (a real geographic place), which is where covert operations by the thief had been suspected. Because the agent on the field did not have time to analyze the samples herself, we were instructed to be extremely careful in the handling of the ice. It was clear that in each sample there was something embedded in the ice, and it was the agent's mission to reveal the hidden objects. With straws and some lukewarm water available to use, agents had to figure out how to melt their individual ice samples in less than 30 minutes without touching the ice or the water with their hands.

This was an inquiry-based program, so any input from me was few and far between, allowing for the agents to lead the conversations. Deception Island is a small island on the coast of Antarctica, a place that the agents knew nothing about. Their first plan of action was to go to the giant $9' \times 14'$ world map covering the entire west wall and locate the island. On the package that the agents in Antarctica sent the ice samples in (and that was available for the agents to view), an address was given along with the coordinates. Using this information, the agents were able to read the latitude and longitude numerical values on the map and locate the island, which was no small feat considering NONE of them could name, let alone locate, the continents just two weeks prior. Seeing that the island was white on the map, as opposed to the green and brown colors of the other continents, the agents were able to deduce that it was an island covered in ice. After this, they moved to the tables, where they began experimenting with the supplies provided to try and melt the ice.

Aside from not being able to touch the ice or water with their hands, they could not use their mouths either (which is what many of the older kids were immediately inclined to do; suck up the water and spit it out). By listening to the older kids boisterously talk about how to melt the ice, one of our youngest agents got an idea. The four-year-old girl figured out that she could scoop up (albeit very little) water from one cup with the straw and quickly transfer it to her ice sample. The other agents all congratulated her on her brilliance and got to work. After a few minutes of this, one of the third-grade agents figured out that if you plug the top of the straw with your finger or hand and then "carried" the water over to your ice sample, you could remove your finger/hand and release the water held in the straw. This theory allowed for more water to be transferred, which in turn melted the ice faster.

Once the gems were revealed (there were three gems per sample), they had to analyze them and determine what type of stone they were. Books on gems were on hand as well as a "gem map" and a digital microscope. Once the gems were correctly identified, the agents were able to keep them as a token of good faith from the Free Library of Philadelphia

Espionage Agency (FLPEA) for their hard work and loyalty to the agency. Side note: The gems were plastic and came in a package of about 500 for less than $10. This activity was STEM based, and interconnected several disciplines, all in a manner that was applicable for students ranging in age from three to sixteen. It was inquiry at work, and it was beautiful. The STEM breakdown for this activity is as follows:

Skills Used	Description
Science	Earth sciencephysics used in the transfer of water, discussing how water can have various states (solid, liquid, and gas) and determining the temperature at which water turns from liquid to solid
Technology	Computer literacy with the use of the digital microscope
Engineering	Design and implementation of their contraption to transfer water from one cup to another
Math	Reading longitude and latitude coordinates on the world map, as well as reading temperature levels on a mercury-in-glass thermometer

Some added interdisciplinary bonus points are the following:

Skills Used	Description
Geography	Location and description of Deception Island
History	Discussing the various things scientists have found embedded in ice (such as fossils) and how the island got its name
Literacy	Reading through the mission sheet and gem description, and writing their observations of the gemstones down on their forms
Teamwork	Collaborating together on reading the world map and figuring out how to transfer water as well as working together to identify the gemstones

As you can see, there are so many different aspects of learning that went into that one activity, with one of the most important being that the agents had fun. At one point, when the agents were all around the tables dutifully transferring lukewarm water onto their ice samples, one of the fourth graders piped up and told the group that the temperature at which water freezes is 32 degrees. A few others chimed in saying they knew that too, and that they had even noticed that we had a thermometer on the window near where I kept the toys. The chatter died down, and after a few seconds one of the second graders piped up and said, "Hey! This is kind of like science!" *Oh, no!* I thought, *I've been found out! Now that they know I have an educational motive, they're going to stop and quit the club!* Thankfully, another agent came to my rescue and retorted with "Yeah, except this is actually fun!" *Phew!*

Studies show that we're headed toward an uncertain future (as if any future is certain, but you get my gist) for at the current rate we as a nation are not producing enough qualified people to fill STEM-specific roles in the workforce. There will be a deficit, and it is being traced back to the lack of exposure to STEM at an early age, even as early as preschool. The lack of confidence that students, specifically girls, have when it comes to science, technology, engineering, and math is being linked to teachers who are not confident in those areas and curriculums that don't address those disciplines until the later grades, which for many is too little and too late.

With the onset of technology that is progressing at what seems to be the speed of light, we are becoming more and more reliant on scientists, technicians, engineers, and mathematicians to keep us up to date. After-school programs, libraries, camps, churches, and clubs are all attempting to stay relevant by jumping on the STEM bandwagon and offering programs based on these four disciplines. Recently, I attended a webinar on how to incorporate STEM into public programs in the children's department of libraries. I went in with high hopes, but was disappointed to find that their idea of STEM programming was to offer the latest STEM books in STEM-related displays. Although I have no doubt that their intentions are all very good and well, the problem is that simply offering books is not enough. There needs to be a practical application that links the information in books to something that the students are able to participate in. Another problem that many run into with interdisciplinary and STEM-focused style of programming is that because there is so much to cover with the multiple fields, there is less time to dig down deep into specific disciplines. It's a shallow skimming of a very wide pond.

Recognizing the Educational Content in All That You Do

It always irks me to hear people refer to general fields of work as "STEM related." *She works in a STEM field as a mechanical engineer. He is steeped in STEM as a computer programmer.* Almost every job and/or activity involves STEM in one way or another, making everything STEM related. Take professional soccer for example. This role typically isn't associated with STEM, yet from the Magnus Effect (the curved path a soccer ball follows when flying through the air) to calculating the speed at which a soccer ball travels when kicked, all four STEM disciplines are involved.

Don't get me wrong, I fully understand that certain fields have a heavier emphasis on STEM, while others lean toward the humanities or arts, but what I'm suggesting is that STEM is all around us and in everything that we do. Rather than focus on incorporating those four disciplines *into* your programs, try shifting your train of thought and think about how you can pull the STEM concepts *out of* your content. There is something to be learned from everything, so don't shy away from presenting a baking program because it doesn't have enough educational content to substantiate it with all of the other high school and college prep programs. There is PLENTY of STEM involved in baking, believe me; I helped to run my family's bakery for a few years and I was positively steeped in calculations (money handling, budgets, etc.), new technologies (registers, walk-in ovens, etc.), and science (ruining an entire batch of bread because I didn't factor in the humidity when allowing the dough to rise), just to name a few examples.

When you take the focus off of creating something that is overtly STEM-centric, then it will allow you to think more freely about what kind of program you want to offer. As librarians, there is a certain level of expectancy that comes from the public in regard to your own knowledge about ALL things. You need to know about volcanoes? Ask a librarian. You need help with your report on President Carter that's due in 10 hours and all of the books you need have been checked out? Ask a librarian. Your toilet is burping up mystery chunks? Ask a librarian. Librarians are like walking, talking, real-life search engines, and though it's a compliment to have so much knowledge assumed, it's misplaced. While many of you may very well know why volcanoes go dormant, what President Carter's legacy is, and how to intervene in rogue toilet behavior, what librarians are best at (and really, what they're there for) is leading people to reliable sources so they can then educate themselves. For the programming librarian, not only must you be able to point to information, but as we just discussed, you must be able to bring concepts to life and *pull out* information/knowledge from them.

STEM skills are highly sought after in just about every club or organization imaginable that targets elementary through high school students, but it's important to remember that there are other equally important skills to sharpen. Literacy skills such as print motivation, narrative skills, vocabulary, and phonological awareness all lend themselves nicely to the library environment. Encouraging students to read is at the heart of what all librarians do, and in offering programs for your patrons, you can easily display and offer books related to the topic at hand for checking out or browsing. No matter what kind of program I offer, be it passive or short or long term, I try and have a good variety of books to point kids to in order to foster print motivation. I find that I have to do very little "selling" of the books, as the programs themselves speak to the content, so the books are validated by association alone!

Narrative skills are also rather easy to encourage as children, I have found, are inclined to speak in a story-minded manner. Ask them what they did at recess and you'll most likely get a long-winded and fully detailed glimpse into the wildly colorful life of the young. Encouraging narrative skills is a fabulous way to get parents/guardians involved in their children's learning process. By modeling for parents how to ask questions and encourage detailed responses in children (see Chapter 3), they will begin to pick up on said techniques and begin to implement them at home. At the start of each spy club meeting, I would ask one agent to give a recap of what had happened thus far in the case and where we stood with our thief at large. This became a coveted position, as kids were eager to show how much they were invested in the agency. Those not chosen for the recap were allowed time to fill in gaps and add details that had not yet been mentioned. All of this helped to reinforce narrative skills.

One of the things that shocked me most about the spy club was the rate at which the students increased their vocabularies. You must remember that the students I was working with were less than enthusiastic about school, homework, and learning in general. Out of all of them, only one was somewhat excited about studying for spelling tests, and that was only because I had her do karate moves with each letter that she called out. Each week I introduced new and increasingly difficult/complex words with the mission introductions. Since agents were reading these aloud to one another, and each had his or her own mission sheet to fill out, they were forced to confront the new words. For many of the words, it was a group activity sounding them out, and then inferring the meaning from the context in which it stood. A few times, with particularly difficult words, they asked for help and I gave them another example of the word in a sentence. I then inserted these words in later mission statements for retention and repetition. These new words bubbled over and spilled onto the students' everyday lives, so that when playing games or sitting at the computers, it became common to hear things such as "let me *analyze* your castle" or "this game is *foreign* to me."

As the world continues to progress and change, so must we as a species. The new skills required in the envisioned future are flexibility/adaptability, initiative, self-direction, teamwork/collaboration, critical thinking, problem solving, diversity, creativity, and innovation. Granted, these skills are and have been required of people present and past, but there is a greater emphasis on instilling these competencies at younger and younger ages. It also helps when compiling your professional portfolios to be able to list specific skills taught with each program you have listed.

Incorporating learning standards used in your local school systems will also bring legitimacy to the programs that you offer.

In order to start thinking in regard to the aforementioned skills in the programs that you offer, I encourage you to begin picking out the skill sets required in the activities that you observe kids doing and/or the activities that you yourself take part in. For instance, I do a lot of cycling with a major group ride every summer (20,000+ riders going for 500 miles over seven days). The group ride incorporates every skill mentioned earlier, and to illustrate, I've created a graph (similar to what I do with my library programs).

Skills Used	Description
Flexibility and adaptability	The ability to change gear, clothes, and attitudes as the weather changed (rain, cold, wind, etc.)
Initiative and self-direction	Training throughout the year, leading up to the ride (log 1,000 miles on your own before the ride)
Teamwork and collaboration	It takes MASSIVE amounts of teamwork and collaboration to ride side by side with 20,000 riders. Calling out, "on your left" as you pass by, helping one another when bikes malfunction, first aid/CPR for hurt riders, and so on.
Critical thinking and problem solving	Trying to find your tent in a sea of people/bikes/tents without cell phones
Diversity	On this ride, no matter what political party you affiliate with, where you're from, whom you love, what you do, or what you think, we're all riders on a 500-mile journey
Creativity and innovation	Jerry-rigging extra water bottles, speakers, and other accoutrements to bicycles to get through the long days
STEM	**Science**: Life science. From saddle sores to severe sunburn, there are a variety of things to know about how the body reacts to riding a bicycle for extended periods of time **Technology**: GPS tracking devices on bikes. New bike technology (carbon frames, deep wheel sets, etc.) **Engineering**: Bike maintenance **Math**: Speed, distance, elevation climb/descent calculation
Print motivation	Riders seek out maps of the area in which we're riding, as well as books related to the ride, cycling, camping, and towns we pass through
Narrative skills	At the end of each day, there is a ritual of telling the nonriders (support vehicle teams) what happened out on the road during the ride
Vocabulary	In my very first year of riding, I learned the following terms: Rumbles: grooves in the pavement SAG: Support and Gear Kybo: port-a-potty

Valuable skills that can be pulled from programs go way beyond the sets that I've already listed. Geography, map reading, foreign language, cultural competency, local history, and zoology are just some of the few areas in which students can gain knowledge. Thinking in broad terms like this will allow you to host programs that are SO much more than STEM. They're interdisciplinary, relevant, and fun programs that are holistic at heart and will serve to help create global citizens that are well rounded. A loft promise, I know, but the opportunities that libraries have in assisting with the upbringing of our new generations and further educating the established generations can have a great impact on individuals, the community, and the world at large.

Joining Forces with the Maker Movement

I could feel myself turning green with envy as I went on a virtual tour of a public school's maker space. Power tools sparkled as they caught the fluorescent lights beaming and humming from above. Circuit boards, LEDs, and monitors lined the walls and countertops. Projects from students stood tall and proud atop the cabinets. *Lucky*, I thought to myself. *Lucky to have a budget and time to create a space like that.* For a while I completely dismissed the idea of joining in the maker movement, because there simply wasn't enough money, time, or space to have something so grand and magnificent as a maker space.

A few weeks later, as I rolled out the after-school cart, which was loaded down with origami, construction and printer paper, glue, scissors, googly eyes, tape, markers, crayons, pencils, toilet paper tubes, straws, and any other low-cost, bulk item we had lying around the building, I realized that we were knee-deep in the maker movement! These kids were making new things all of the time, with what little resources I offered them. Just because we didn't have fancy power tools or tablets for them to create code on didn't mean that they weren't part of what makes a maker a maker. The ability to look at individual pieces, envision a new product, and bring the said product to fruition is at the heart of the maker movement, and I was very pleased to discover that it took very little financial commitment. Of course, LEDs, robots, and power tools are all very exciting and lend themselves nicely to the making of something, but they're not necessary in fostering the spirit of a maker.

With this realization, I encouraged making every single day and incorporated it into the spy club missions. As mentioned earlier, one of the greatest ways to implement successful programming is to piggyback off of something that is already established and doing well. The maker movement has been sweeping across libraries like a wildfire. Everywhere I look, I see webinars, conferences, books, and blogs, all gushing about the staying power and transformative change that maker spaces bring to libraries. With as little as some paper and tape, you can turn your department into a maker space. In order to keep messes under control (relatively speaking of course), I tend to keep maker areas relegated to a table or two. It's amazing what kids can come up with when given some supplies and let loose. The entire spy club was kick-started with a spy phone made out of a piece of paper!

Many of the concepts and skills associated with maker spaces lean heavily toward STEAM. The added "art" component of maker spaces comes from the creativity and art mindfulness required when making something look appealing. Sure, paper airplanes can be made out of white A4 paper, but what will set it apart from the others is how it looks once decorated. Perhaps, one will create his or her own logo to go on the side of the plane. Or, maybe someone will draw the pilot, crew, and passengers, all looking out of the windows! This sense of creativity and design will help to enhance the STEM concepts.

Though I had my maker cart out each day for the kids to use, it never really took off until I incorporated it with the spy club. During one mission, the agents were told that a fellow agent in the field in Antarctica had been stranded. A new raft design was needed that would sustain high winds for him to make an escape to the tip of South America. The maker cart was brought out, and using two gutters lined with plastic garbage bags capped at the ends and filled with water, the agents got to work, designing their rafts. Once they had a prototype (new vocabulary word for most of them), we would set their raft down in one end of the gutter, turn on a fan that sat up against the same end of the gutter to simulate the high winds that whip through the Drake Passage (geography lesson), and see how far the raft would go. Some sank immediately, before we even had a chance to turn on the fan. Others didn't sink, but they didn't budge either. There wasn't enough surface area to catch the wind and travel down to the other end. The goal was for your raft to successfully float from one end of the gutter to the other, and after many trials and errors we finally had two agents succeed. Their designs were then sent to headquarters and forwarded on to the agent in Antarctica.

The maker mind-set behind this mission was prevalent, and didn't require the high-tech gadgetry that often comes to mind when thinking of a maker space. Even if I had high-tech equipment and power tools and all the bells and whistles, I would still have hesitated to incorporate them into this activity. When you're given basic and limited supplies to create something as complex as a raft that floats, travels, and sustains high winds, you are forced to think in innovative and creative ways, as well as manage your resources. If these kids can master those skills while creating and making things with limited low-tech supplies, then imagine how adept and successful they will be when presented with supplies from the other end of the spectrum.

Many times I have seen maker spaces set out for kids, teens, and even adults with no context. What I mean by this is that the doors have been flown open and the only directive is to come in and make something. For a handful of the population, this may be all the kick they need. Their wheels are already turning and access to this type of environment and supply list is exactly what they needed to bring their ideas to fruition. For some, perhaps they just need to come in and tinker for a while before inspiration hits. For others, they will need a little more direction before the wheels begin to turn.

From my experience working with kids, I found that they usually need some kind of nudge to get started, which is where the structure and storyline of a program come in handy. Marrying a program with a maker space is really the best-case scenario for both concepts, as it gives context to the maker cart/area while simultaneously fostering a maker mentality with your participants as well as yourself. For a recent event that I was a part of, we were in need of a simple letter cipher. Rather than going out and buying one, which could have been pricy, the leaders of the program used our 3D printer to design and print their own ciphers right there in-house! To model a maker mind-set for your peers and patrons will not only inspire them, but it will also show off what you and your tools are capable of.

DIY (do-it-yourself) has been a huge trend for decades, and a maker cart is the manifestation of that same mentality. Though I did use the cart during certain missions, it was the daily access to it that made a big difference in the lives of the kids. Many school project posters were made using materials from the maker cart, and all the better they were for it. Everything from testing the power of flight with paper airplanes, kites, and parachutes to exploring the ins and outs of poetry were magnified with the maker cart and what it had to offer.

Just like you would take inventory of your supplies to use in a program, so too must you know what your maker space entails. If you've got some circuit boards available, then you should know how many, what accouterments go with them, and how to use them. If there is a limited number of items, then factor that into the program development. I'm hosting a program for upper elementary–aged kids in a few months and want to incorporate some circuits that my library purchased. We only have enough materials for one light-censored remote switch to be made. With five days and 30 kids, this would not suffice to only have one item. Rather than putting them in groups and rotating the circuit boards (a viable option), I created the light-censored remote switch and turned it into one of the components that will be used in the program. The kids won't get the chance to build their own circuit, but they will get to see it in action and will be given the opportunity for further examination of the circuit during the program. If I had a dozen of these kits, then I would have loved to give them to the kids to build their own, but I don't, so I took what I did have and made it work.

If the program that you're developing requires any kind of component, then first see if you can make it yourself. Exemplify the maker mentality and experiment with supplies readily available. To have something that is low cost and easily replaceable will take the stress away from a student breaking an expensive item. It will also go to show your students that they can make similar components of their own at home. The maker space isn't limited to a specific geographic area; rather it's a mentality that can be applied to all that you do.

One of my favorite maker moments with the spy club came when our mission "took us" to outer space. The agents had intercepted a letter from the thief written in pigpen, decoded the cipher, and discovered that they were "headed to the Crab." Immediately the agents went to the stacks and began searching through the books on crabs and other crustaceans. Finding nothing, they inquired with the head adult librarian and she (who, of course, was an agent in the FLPEA herself) told them about nebulae. Off to the books on space they went, and voila! There on the shelf one of the books filled with images taken from the Hubble Telescope had an FLPEA marker (logo) on its spine. The kids frantically flipped through the pages, reading aloud what a nebula was with their voices getting higher and higher until they reached the climactic moment of discovering that one such nebula was called the CRAB!

The basement had been set up with a flight simulator (we did a lot of simulation), and the agents were tasked with designing and creating a rocket ship that would fly through "space," dodging the black holes and "land on" the Crab Nebula. Everything about this mission was of the maker mind-set. I had created the flight simulation using string, tissue paper, and LED lights. For the black holes, I balled up black tissue paper and hung them at various heights throughout the room. Stars were smaller sections of yellow tissue paper, with a few of them equipped with an LED at the center to shine and twinkle. Three nebulae were made with a variety of colored tissue paper and LEDs stuck throughout to represent new stars being born. All of the "space matter" was hanging at various heights throughout the room, and once the agents had created their rockets, they were to stand at one end of the room and attempt to "fly" (throw) their ship to "land on" (touch) the Crab Nebula. If their ship hit a star or a black hole, then they had failed and needed to wait their turn and try again (to control the chaos, only two ships were allowed to launch at a time).

Aside from introducing the simulator and counting down the rocket launches, I stood back and observed the agents. Many of them initially made simple paper airplanes, but after failures to launch and/or getting sucked into black holes, they went back to the drawing board. Going back to Chapter 2, where we talked about creating a safe space for failure, a major part of the scientific method is testing your hypothesis, which often requires troubleshooting. If at first your experiment doesn't give you results, then try, try again. There is no shame in failing. It's part of the process! When the paper airplanes fell short of reaching the Crab Nebula, the agents started working on new designs for their space craft. Cylindrical, square, and even triangular space crafts were created, tested, altered, and tested again until they were able to reach their destination.

Combining a maker mind-set with a stellar program creates something larger and more magnificent than either could accomplish on its own. When you're not able to infuse a storyline or a program with a maker area/cart, you can still foster a learning environment by having materials accessible. Much like I did with my cart full of supplies available to the kids on a daily basis, so too can you provide materials for creative and innovative thinking. To give some inspiration each day I had a sample product on display made out of the materials that were available for that particular day. More often than not, this example was just a starting point and the kids' products went way beyond what I had initially made.

I'm a big believer in individual thought, and am conscious about the child who doesn't thrive in group environments. As a shy child myself who internalized much of my thought process, a passive maker cart would have appealed to me much more than an organized club or program. For many children, a simple example of a paper aircraft with supplies and books to help them in their own creative making process would be just as effective as the flight simulator was. Being mindful of your patrons and their different learning styles means offering different types of programs and opportunities to interact with information/knowledge. It also fosters a sense of diversity and inclusion by recognizing one another's differences and making everyone feel welcome.

In the beginning of this book I mentioned that the majority of people stop playing at an early age. This is also true of making. Children are inclined to making things of a wide variety, partly because they can't go out and buy whatever they want and partly because they have imaginations that make up for what the item lacks. In-between my junior and senior year in undergrad, I spent the summer nannying a six-year-old boy. The majority of my time with him was spent as pirates sailing the seven seas, searching for lost treasure and fighting off the British army. We had a fully equipped tall ship complete with a gang-plank, troves of treasure used for bartering, telescopes for keeping a lookout for the Brits, and swords for when we finally came face-to-face with the army. All of this, *all of it*, was made out of cardboard. We had spent almost two solid weeks constructing this elaborate world, taking over just about every room in the house and exhausting their back stock of cardboard boxes.

We could have gone out and purchased cheap handheld telescopes, pirate booty, and perhaps even a plastic pirate ship, but that would take away from the teamwork required to build this set the individuality in the end product, and it wouldn't have forced us to think critically about how to construct something that resembles a tall ship (this boat was six feet tall and had doors, windows, and a steering mast). We became closer through the process and learned so much more than we would have browsing the isles of shops. The ability to make is what makes humans so extraordinary. It's why monkeys and llamas aren't constructing their own rockets and taking space walks on the moon. Sure, there are some species that use tools, but humans make and we are good at it. Just take a look around you. It's amazing what we as a species have been able to come up with, and we're just getting started. If you haven't already, then join in the movement—the maker movement!

The BIG Picture

Odds are that the programs you're currently offering, whether they're story times or coding clubs, are already steeped in STEAM. Taking time to recognize this will validate the work you're doing and perhaps inspire you to infuse more STEAM and/or twenty-first-century skills into your events. Regardless of whether or not you've got a maker space at your building, you can enrich your programs by having a maker mind-set and inspiring the same thought process in others.

Reflection Questions

1. In what ways can you incorporate STEAM and twenty-first-century skills into your programs?
2. Think back to the last program you participated in. What STEAM and twenty-first-century skills were knowingly/unknowingly taught?
3. In your own words, define a "maker mind-set." Once completed, think about how you can bring your maker mind-set to your day-to-day work as well as your programs.

CHAPTER 7

Grabbing and Holding Participants' Attention

Marketing and Promotion

Before my spy club ever began, I was dropping hints and small seeds of intrigue that I later reaped 10-fold. From the very first week of the school year when I made the spy phone, the kids and I played a running game of *Secret Agent* that lasted up until I began the club. I continued with my role as a spy for the library, and as I got closer to launching my program, I began confiding in my students about something happening within the agency. I was always vague about what was going on, but I began weaving the tapestry of my storyline so that by the time I announced that applications for membership were open, there was already a sense of mystery and adventure for me to build upon. These were my initial marketing tactics, and it worked. The rest, I left up to the agents.

A few weeks into the program I had two girls come dashing into the library on "spy club day" to tell me that Daniel should hereby be officially removed and banned from the Free Library of Philadelphia Espionage Agency (FLPEA). Quite a bold statement to lead off with, but I heard them out and they reasoned that he should be stripped of his membership because they had overheard him telling his friend about spy club on the bus. A few moments later, Daniel came shuffling into the library, tears streaming down his face as he approached me for what he was sure to be his removal from the agency. My heart absolutely melted as I knelt down to his eye level and calmly asked him if what the girls were telling me was true. He nodded. I asked him if he remembered the application and oath to secrecy that he signed when applying to become an agent. He did. Of course, I wasn't going to kick him out of the club; in fact he was doing me a great service by spreading the word, but he did sign a contract and with that came responsibility—something I was trying to teach to these kids in addition to the STEM, literacy, and twenty-first-century skills. I used this moment to teach a twofold lesson. First, I reassured Daniel that he was a valued agent and that we needed him on the case. However, he needed to keep in mind the document that he had signed his name to. I asked if he thought whether or not his friends he had spoken to were trustworthy, and he eagerly responded that they were. The next week, Daniel was prouder than a peacock as he watched his friend and his friend's little brother fill out the application form and be accepted into the FLEPA. The second lesson to be learned from this situation was with the girls and their whistle-blowing. Again, in the application they signed, it was stated that, "I will be respectful, and work together with my fellow agents." We talked about how rather than running to me to tell on Daniel, they could have approached him, their fellow agent, and reminded him of the document he signed and the sensitive nature of the mission.

My point is that by giving the kids something that they were proud of and felt a sense of belonging to, they couldn't help but bubble and gush about it wherever they went. Once the kids were accepted into the agency, they were given an official ID card with their alias as well as a magnetic pin with the FLPEA logo—similar to the pins the secret service agents wear. These pins were worn by the kids everywhere, and they were worn with a sense of pride that was on par with the Chicago Cub's after winning the World Series. These pins, which were so graciously donated by a trophy shop, were far more effective than any poster I could have produced and pinned up at local shops. Several schools were represented at my branch, and when the kids wore their pins to class, it was like having dozens of little marketing agents walking around everyday, all day in three different locations.

I had branded my club with that FLPEA logo, a simple design I came up with in Photoshop. In this day and age of social media, branding is an important step in the marketing process. How do you brand? First of all, you have some type of logo, slogan, or catchphrase to represent the organization you're a part of. For many people, the library's logo will be the only thing you need. Second, you must be consistent with the logo/slogan. Don't mess around with type font or change up the wording. It must be the same, always. This helps to *brand* the logo into patrons' minds. Third, put it on absolutely everything. Any piece of paper, space, or item used in my spy club was accompanied by the logo. The kids immediately associated that image with the club, which was synonymous with the Free Library of Philadelphia. Though I didn't use the FLP's logo on any of my material, I didn't have to because the kids all knew that this spy group was a subcommunity of the library.

Traditional media are another great way to market your program. Program guides, local papers, radio stations, fliers at grocery stores, and so on are all effective, though you need to keep your time frame and budget in mind when venturing out to spread the word. Again, it's imperative to utilize your brand when creating these materials. With this type of marketing and promotion, you're more likely to reach the adult caregivers of the children or youth you're trying to reach. With this in mind, use key words that will catch the adult's attention, so that they in turn will bring their children to the library. Knowing your community and their needs will greatly benefit you when marketing to them. What words will trigger their interest? *Free? STEM? College-prep? Coding? After-school program?*

Testimonials from patrons is another great marketing tool, and it's one that I personally value above any marketing that an institution does. When looking for restaurants and auto shops, and even when deciding which graduate program to attend, I went straight to the testimonials and reviews. These reviews and testimonials can make or break any organization. If I come across a glowing review of the new menu item at a cafe that is not on my usual route to and from work, then I may very well go out of my way just to try this item that is being raved about. On the flip side, if I read a bad review that reveals the dark side of how a product is made, then odds are I will steer clear of it. We've begun to institute a practice of gathering positive written testimonials at my current library. Any time a patron comes up to one of the staff to give a compliment or gush about something he or she likes that we're doing/offering, then we'll offer the patron the opportunity to write those good vibes down on a comment card. These comments are then used on our social media sites, program guides, and various other print materials.

Aside from having a stellar program, creating eye-catching posters, and reaching out to the radio station, your greatest marketing and promotion tool will be your established reputation in the community. Just like local businesses get out and mingle with the neighborhood by sponsoring and/or having people from the company establishing a presence and putting a face with the brand, libraries too should follow suit. Get out and mingle with your patrons, who are very likely your own neighbors, and show them that the library is interested in them on a holistic level, not just when they need help logging into their e-mail or writing a report on why fish fart. Get out and show them that librarians are real people, and are also members of the society that they serve. Relationships are a two-way street, and for a library to have a healthy and long-lasting relationship with the community that it resides in, it must actively be a part of the community.

I'm not sure how it happened, but word about the spy club reached the local paper in Philadelphia. A reporter contacted me and asked to come and observe a meeting and interview a few kids who were in the program. "Only if," I said, "you're in on it." The reporter was given an official ID badge along with a FLPEA pin to wear on his lapel, for this would be the first indicator that my agents would look for in verifying the reporter's identity and legitimacy. He was introduced as an agent sent from headquarters to report on our status with the case, and the following week, when the story broke I received phone calls and e-mails left and right about applications to join in the cryptex hunt! Because I was the only adult leading this program, and I was just about busting at the seams with 30 kids each week, I never did any advertising of my own. Had the program started off slowly, I would have gone out and plastered fliers at the local shops as well as gone into the schools to talk about library services and the Tuesday night spy club.

There is no set way to market, so let your creativity fly! If you've got a new idea that you think will reach your target audience, then by all means (so long as you've got department approval) go for it! I've seen librarians dress up as slices of pizza and go into schools for assemblies to promote their summer reading programs, and the kids ate it up (pun intended). Other libraries have partnered with local bars and created drink coasters with literary trivia questions and the library logo printed on them, all with the hope of getting more adult foot traffic in the library. Guess what? It worked!

The possibilities for coming up with creative, practical, and successful marketing campaigns are endless. The only warning that I have for you is to follow through with what you promise. If you're advertising fun and exciting games, then you'd better have fun and exciting games. If it's a

STEM-based program, then make sure you're able to check off all four disciplines when reviewing the program content. Marketing and promotion don't have to be this imposing and dreaded task. If you love marketing, then more power to you. If, like me, you're not naturally inclined to toot your own horn, then take a look at what other successful organizations are doing to promote their materials and borrow some of their tactics. Ben Bizzle's *Start a Revolution: Stop Acting Like a Library* is a great resource to turn to when diving into the world of marketing and promotion. When we get down to the nitty-gritty, a well-developed program will market itself, as people—especially kids—tend to talk and spread the word about exciting things going on.

Developing a Sense of Ownership

Aside from all of the quantifiable things that the kids learned throughout the spy club (new vocabulary words, skill sets, etc.), I believe that what kept the kids coming back and what had the greatest impact on them in the long term was the sense of ownership they had over the club. It wasn't Miss Rose's spy club (they called me by my middle named rather than my first) or the library's spy club; it was *their* spy club. If I were to liken the club to a business, the closest resemblance would be a co-op. Yes, there were higher powers who ran the show and kept things organized (headquarters), but the members were the owners and they felt proud to be such. This sense of ownership spilled over onto the children's department in the library. It was *their* library, *their* after-school program, and *their* safe space.

Like a proud parent, I had a refrigerator mentality, meaning that when anyone brought me school work that they were proud of, I would hang it on the wall for all to see. I got the feeling that this was not always the case in their home lives, so I was eager to give them positive affirmation for their efforts during their time with me. I started out with a small bulletin board to hang things on, but as this effort gained traction, I had to expand to more and more space, until the entire wall was being used to showcase the students' work. Seeing themselves acknowledged and appreciated in such a tangible way made the kids feel "at home" and like they truly belonged. First-time visitors were drawn to this display wall, and would get a taste of what it was like at our branch just by looking at the work shown. This showed both adults and children that we celebrated our patrons and valued their presence, and that the library was *theirs*. I cannot say enough about the power of giving people a sense of ownership, or at the very least a deep sense of belonging to the institutions they're a part of. Pride, responsibility, and a genuine interest in and appreciation of the organization are just a few of the many benefits that come with this sense of ownership.

As a librarian, this is built into the way that most of us function. Public libraries are created by communities for communities. Adults feel this ownership because the taxes that they pay give them a sense of ownership in the library. This sense, or mentality, that I'm talking about giving to young patrons is not the feeling of ownership that many adult patrons feel over libraries simply because they pay taxes. Just the other day I had a man approach me at the reference desk and comment that it was good to see so many people working and putting his hard-earned tax monies to use. No. This is not what I'm referring to, for the last thing any of us needs is a gaggle of kids talking down to us with an owner–help staff attitude.

So, how then do we foster this deep sense of belonging, without tipping the scale and turning students into mini-dictators who run the joint? First of all, I never used the word "ownership" when talking with them. I never said that the spy materials or the club itself belonged to them. What I did do was step aside as the "all-knowing informant" and allowed them to guide the program. They decided how to address the missions (with some built-in guidance from me), they wrote up all the mission reports, and they gave the interviews when reporters and senior agents came calling. It was all *about* them.

The key word here is *sense*; giving students a *sense* of ownership will greatly impact the odds of them sticking with the program and coming back for repeat visits. When they are so heavily invested in something, as an owner typically is, then they are more inclined to see it through to fruition. Inquiry-based learning (discussed in Chapter 1) is the easiest way to foster this feeling of belonging and importance. It levels the playing ground and takes away the hierarchy that is what makes up much of the formal education we have today. Teachers know it all, and are imparting this knowledge to their pupils. Can kids feel like they belong, or are they heavily invested in environments like that? Absolutely. Some students thrive on that kind of atmosphere. For others, and for short-term programs that aren't mandatory five-days-a-week programs, shifting the focus onto the kids and allowing them to lead the discussion and investigation of the topic at hand will speed up this process and get them invested quickly. They are the ones asking the questions and suggesting possible solutions or new directions to go in, and it's hard to lose attention when you're involved in the conversation/action.

For younger patrons, instilling a deep sense of belonging involves reflecting them in how you present your content. For story times with groups of young children I choose books to read aloud that are short and not too verbose. Squirms and wiggles begin to bubble up with the age group rather quickly, and rather than continuously asking them to *sit back down, please* or reminding them that *we need to keep our clothes on when we're at the library*, I have them up singing and dancing, moving, and shaking about every six to nine minutes. Immediately after dancing to a song (of which I am also bouncing around and shaking my own sillies out), I quickly catch my own breath and then read a story to them while they're able to focus and listen for a few minutes. By the time that book is over and done with, there may be time for a quick flannel, but if not, then I've got the next song amped up and ready to go!

This is *their* story time. It is designed and performed specifically for *them*. Though they can't verbalize this feeling yet, they understand the concept, thus feeling like they have a place and a role to play at the library. I often see children leading their caretakers back to the children's department, walking with confidence and determination back to their favorite spot. They know where the toy train set is and where the puppets are, and that we behind the reference desk have a magical power to track down and locate all the Peppa Pig books in the building.

A lot of this is a recap of what we've already discussed. If you're able to foster a safe space, listen and know your audience, tell a good story, and allow them to learn a thing or two along the way, then holding their attention will not be a problem.

Supporting the Classroom

The beauty of working with young patrons is that you have a golden opportunity to build upon what they're already steeped in within the walls of their classroom(s). Whether it's a public, private, or homeschool setting, offering programs that enhance what the children are already learning, in a way that they're not currently learning, will allow them to look at their topic in a new light and with renewed enthusiasm. Case in point: math.

I know there are people out there who are excited about and devote their entire lives to the study of math. I am not one of these people, nor were any of the kids I was working with in Philadelphia. The most immediate need that these kids had, and why almost all of them came to the library in the first place, was to get help with their homework. I tried my best to make this a fun and interesting activity, with karate-chop spelling practice and acting out history lessons, but their math lessons threw me for a loop. It's been a while since I myself was an elementary school student, and though math is math, meaning two plus two still equals four, the way in which they were teaching it has changed drastically. This new math is meant to get students thinking about numbers in a way that lends itself to coding, which is where many jobs are headed to in the future. Trying to walk these kids through the new math without reverting to the old math, *my math*, was akin to herding a pack of angry cats through a mud pit. It was frustrating and we were all a mess and exhausted when it was said and done.

The curriculum writers tried to dress up the homework sheets by adding fun graphics and interesting blurbs that gave reason behind this new way of thinking. One day, while reading one such blurb, I learned that this "new method" wasn't so new after all, and was inspired by the ancient South American quipu (kee-poo), a series of knots on strings used for counting and storytelling. Finding this interesting, I read it aloud to the table and was met with no response. They could not have cared any less about where this infuriating math came from.

Fast forward six months later to the second week of spy club. The previous week the agents had analyzed evidences collected from the crime scene, some of which were foreign coins, and determined that the thief was headed to South America. Having submitted this information to headquarters, senior officials were able to get an agent on the field. Based on the information that the Andorra agents had given, the field agent was able to beat the thief to his next check-in point. At this location, a quipu was discovered. It was taken, packaged, and sent to Andorra for analysis. The mission statement gave a brief overview of how the quipu was obtained and that ancient people used them to count and tell stories. The agents then decoded the quipu and came up with two Dewey decimal numbers, which led them to their next clue.

While counting out the knots on the strings, one of the fourth graders stopped and turned to look for me. Without moving away from the quipu, which was taped to the wall, she yelled across the room to me saying, "THIS IS WHAT YOU READ ABOUT IN MY MATH BOOK!!" A wave of pure, unadulterated joy washed over both of our faces as she made the connection from real life to her school work. All of the agents clamored to get their turn with the quipu and count out the knot systems to reveal the hidden numbers. But really, what they were clamoring toward was a math lesson. Dividing numbers by groups (ones, tens, hundreds, etc.) and then counting them and writing them in the correct place value on their mission sheets was nothing more than what they were already doing on their homework.

Why were the kids so eager to complete the mission sheets, and so reluctant to do their homework sheets? They were asking for the same types of problems, and both referred back to the ancient quipus. What was the difference? For the answer to that question, all we have to do is look back at the previous chapters of this book.

Chapter Theme	Description
1: Play	The kids were playing a massive, week-long game that revolved around them. Game mechanics such as scavenger hunts, resource management, and risk (to name just a few) were implemented in the weekly missions. They were living and playing a life-sized game, and having the time of their lives.
2: Location	With the program being at the library, they felt safe and free to fail. The pressure of getting things right and keeping grades up was gone, so they were more inclined to try something out. Failure had no ramifications; in fact it was a necessary step in the process to getting it right.
3: Knowing your audience	The activity was age appropriate and directly applicable to what they were learning in the classroom. Using inquiry-based teaching techniques, the kids were in charge of making connections and solving problems that arose.
4: Story	All students were deeply invested in the story. They were main characters in the world of the FLPEA, and uncovering the quipu's message was how they moved the story/mission forward.
5: Details	The quipu mission was a small detail in the grand scope of the entire case. It fit in with the overarching story of the spy club, as well as with their own lives (specifically, their "school story").
6: Education	Math concepts that came directly from their homework sheets were the driving force behind this activity. They were able to utilize the skills they already had and built upon them with a new and hands-on way of exploring the concepts.

Teachers have one of the most difficult jobs on the planet, if you ask me, and anything that outside groups can do to support classroom studies will help to reinforce teachers and their students. In turn, this will help our communities, for the young people of today are the leaders and changemakers of tomorrow. Libraries can assist in amplifying concepts taught in schools as teachers are faced with rigorous standards to adhere to, budgets to deal with, and limited amounts of resources and time to allocate.

For the spy club, most missions were based on broad concepts that the kids had been working on all year, regardless of the grade they were in. There are always core concepts that are underlying in the curriculums being taught across multiple grades: computer literacy, spelling, social skills, teamwork, and so on. Skills that were used in our weekly missions would, and did, translate to the classroom. Many times I had agents come and tell me about how they were able to raise their hand in class and tell the teacher something they had learned while on one of our missions.

As I mentioned earlier, with inquiry-based teaching, the kids were in control of the direction that the activity went in and thus they made their own connections between real life, the classroom, and the spy missions.

The quipu was one of the few exceptions where I took a specific lesson, directly from the textbook, and implemented it in the spy curriculum. Seeing that I had such a wide range of students and abilities with my agents covering such a wide age range, specific classroom concepts were not the most appropriate way to develop the program. Had I gone into more classroom specifics, I would have run the risk of losing a good amount of my agents' interest and concentration. Had I limited the program to one specific age group, everyone would have missed out, even the chosen ones invited to partake in the program. When you've got an interdisciplinary program and a diverse participant group (different ages, genders, backgrounds, etc.), you allow for more learning opportunities and teachable moments. On more than one occasion, the younger agents were able to make a connection that the older kids had not, and by working together, everyone was able to learn something new. For the things that older agents were in the know about, they were quick to call it out and tell the other agents what it was they knew. Kids love to show off, and when it's about having information, then I'm all for it.

Another way that I was able to support the classroom was to introduce topics that were new but that still fell under the broad umbrella of a core discipline. For example, one week the mission required the agents to do a pH test. My very oldest agent was familiar with the periodic table, but for the rest of the group, this was an entirely new concept. It required a bit more interaction on my end, as I had to go into more depth with my introduction of the mission so that they knew what they were doing and not just blindly messing about with the different test tubes full of liquids. Equipped with safety glasses, homemade pH test strips (cabbage-dyed watercolor paper), and a set of test tubes and droppers to test the pH of the liquid they held, this was the first "scienc-y" experiment that many of them had ever done. We talked about lab safety, the periodic table, and the properties of certain elements in addition to how these related to the case of the missing cryptex. Now, were any of them going to be doing pH tests in their science labs at school? Probably not, seeing as several of the schools did not have science labs or equipment. Also, this concept was pretty advanced for the level that most of them were at. Yet, the agents were able to understand the basic concepts of how different elements make up the planet, how things that look similar can have entirely different properties, and how to be safe when using lab equipment and test materials that could potentially be harmful. These are all things that they can take with them and think about when they're in the classroom and science time rolls around. It may be years before any of them are presented with the periodic table in a formal classroom setting, but they'll have an experience to draw upon, which will make their learning all the richer.

If you don't already have a connection with an educator at your local schools, then I highly encourage you to reach out and open a line of communication. You needn't take a lot of each other's time in planning and preparing plans together. On the contrary, simple and short e-mails about what's currently happening in the classroom and at the library may be all that it takes. Knowing that Mr. Craig is teaching his fourth graders about civil rights is all you need to know to make a display that reflects the topic, host a discussion night with local civil rights/social justice activists, or create a program that explores our history of segregation and the power of peaceful protests. Plugging yourself into the local schools, even if only via short e-mails, is a great way to stay relevant in the kid's greater academic life as well as gain the trust and appreciation of parents and teachers.

The BIG Picture

The best form of advertising is by honest, word-of-mouth praise from one patron to another. Don't wait to start being innovative and exciting until your first big program; start now so that people begin talking about how great you and your services are! Once you do get to the program, give the participants a sense of ownership so that they feel invested in and proud of belonging to it. By supporting the classroom in the programs that you offer, you're going above and beyond, as librarians often do, to help the community at large, and for this, you will be appreciated.

Reflection Questions

1. Are your programs exciting enough for kids to talk about at school and home? Yes or no?
2. Are *you* excited enough about your programs to gush about them? Yes or no?
    a) What is the name of the closest school to your building?
    b) Do you currently collaborate with one of the educators there? Yes or no?
    c) How are you supporting the classroom (either with or without educator collaboration)?

CHAPTER 8

How to Get Repeat Visitors

Act Like a Kid, or, It Takes One to Know One

I have two dogs that I rescued when I lived in Houston, Texas: a Texas Brown and a Texas Black, Brix and Ollie, respectively. My family always had a small dog when I was growing up, but it wasn't until I adopted my own that the full responsibility of having a pet hit me. The first thing I did, before I even signed the adoption paperwork, was to gather all the books and information I could on how to properly train a dog. Almost all of the books preached that in order to train a dog, you must think like a dog. It was a bit of an abstract concept for me to try and think like a dog, but ultimately I was able to figure it out, and now, several years later, I have two of the best dogs on the planet. This theory of fully knowing your audience is universal and can be applied to any field of work.

Bankers must think like and be able to anticipate the actions of potential investors and/or borrowers. The same is true for writers and readers, port-a-potty designers and fairgoers, and bar tenders and their thirsty friends. If these people weren't able to channel their inner audience member, then their products would be wildly off target. Picture book authors and illustrators read thousands of picture books to help them understand what it is that children find appealing. They also spend loads of time with children to get an understanding of what their thought process is like and how they interpret stories. I cannot speak about the method of port-a-potty designers, but I trust that there is a method to their madness. I can only imagine how barbaric our portable bathroom systems would be if it weren't for the good souls working to create the right-size "seat," the most friendly "drop depth," and the most efficient drainage hookup. Bar tenders must know what kind of drinks to have on hand, how to lend a good listening ear, and when to cut people off, otherwise they will lose their clientele to the half a dozen other bars within a reasonable distance.

Not only do children's librarians have bookshops and other libraries all vying for kids' attention, but they're up against organized sports, clubs, tutoring, and the million other activities that make up the modern child's schedule. One of the biggest assets of being a library is that programs are free (or involve a minimal charge). However, children's librarians must be able to think and act like a kid in order to appeal to them on all levels.

Starting with a broad view, take a minute to think about your physical building. When designing a space for children and youth, try and imagine what a child would think about your area. How would a sterile environment impact your patrons' attitude and actions, as opposed to a colorful and warm one? The space itself can help facilitate the actions of your students, and will speak to them oftentimes before you or another staff member will utter a word to them. More often than not, children's and teens' bedrooms are colorfully painted and adorned with decorations reflecting their own interests (band posters, pictures of friends, etc.). By looking at your space through the lens of a young patron, you can help to facilitate a welcoming space that will draw people in time and time again.

Let's zoom in a bit on the collections. This is the area in which children's librarians excel beyond measure. The ability to curate a bank of books that appeal to and fulfill the information needs of users is what has kept the children's departments relevant and useful as we've transitioned into a digital age. Books are published at a phenomenal rate, yet children's librarians are able to stay on top of the game and have a deep knowledge about what's available and what's hot. A large portion of this skill is knowing how to think and act like a kid, though you may not realize it. Knowing what your readers will enjoy involves being able to step into their shoes to try and anticipate their needs and desires.

Moving on from what lies inside of the books, it's also helpful to think and act like a kid when considering the binding of books. How do you categorize your picture books? Many of those users are not yet fully literate, and an alphabetical system may prove to be difficult for young readers to figure out. Digital databases and catalog search engines comprise primarily of text, which renders the young and illiterate searcher powerless. Perhaps visual cues via stickers or categorizing books based on themes make more sense for your user community. Pictures may prove to be useful beyond the categorizing of books, by incorporating them on program guides and activity sheets. Shelf placement is another thing to keep in mind when trying to create a learning playground. If your students cannot independently reach the books of their choice, then this may dampen your effectiveness. Although, if a collection re-haul is not within your scope (which, let's be realistic, for most it's not), it's still worthwhile to put yourself into your users' shoes and try to anticipate what they think and act like.

Here's an important question for you: How do you make a tissue dance? You put a little *boogie* in it! I always have a handful of jokes tucked into my mind so that I can pull them out to break the ice with new kids that I meet. By doing something as simple as cracking a corny joke, you can break down walls and have an "in" with people (of all ages—almost everyone is up for a good joke). Not only am I quick to tell a joke, but I'm also quick to laugh at my own as well as at the made-up-on-the-spot and not-so-funny ones that kids tell. I allow my inner child to drive the bus, so to speak, for kids recognize playfulness and uninhibited joy. These are often characteristics that define themselves, and birds of a feather...

Much of this boils down to the attitude you have toward your patrons, which will determine the type of interactions you have. During every single spy club meeting, I was always just as excited as the kids were when they discovered something new. Unchecked joy is contagious, and if you allow yourself to indulge in it, then you are not only sharing an experience with your patrons but also building a bond that will keep them coming back to visit you, use the resources, and attend your programs.

Like a good teacher, you must know where to draw the line. It's true that thinking and acting like a kid will allow you to understand them, thus creating a better environment for them; however, you do have to keep things in line. The ability to balance this friend–role model and child–adult relationship is akin to a high-wire act. Lean too much in one direction and you'll fall off target, either repelling the kids with too many rules and regulations or falling into utter chaos with no one to keep things in check. By establishing ground rules before every program, as well as having general guidelines posted around the building, you can lay the groundwork for an organized and controlled space. As I mentioned earlier, by using language that is positive rather than negative, you can focus on the good behaviors desired rather than the bad ones to be wary of. Infusing creativity in this use of language will break the monotony of rules constantly being shelled out at these kids. *No running* can turn into a game by asking the child if he or she can walk like a bear, or by pretending that he or she is a papa penguin carrying a baby egg between its knees. The infamous *shush* can be revamped by asking kids to use their fox and mice voices. This gets kids thinking about ordinary things in an extraordinary way, which lends itself to a creative and unique environment. If you can swing something like this with the older students, then kudos to you; otherwise a simple conversation rather than a doctoral rule-hashing might get the point across in a stronger way. Incorporating student input with how the space is to be run is another great way to engage the older students with the fundamentals of how the library is run, while giving them that sense of ownership that we discussed in Chapter 7.

During the programs that you host, where the parents and caretakers are in the room with the children, encouraging them to interact with their children and allow their inner kid to come and play will help them build stronger bonds with their children. I'm always amazed at how many adults sit on their phones while expecting me to entertain and teach their children during story time programs. To try and curb this, every time I ask the children to do something (dance, sing, roar, etc.), I also give the adults the same charge. "Kids, roar like a lion! Now grown-ups, it's your turn!" This puts them on the spot, but the look of delight and fits of giggles that ensue quickly wash away any unease the caregivers have for being called out. Seeing me shake my sillies out right along with the kids also emboldens some to get their own groove on and be silly too. Story time is turned into an interactive and exciting activity, which in turn makes the library an interactive and exciting place. A place where kids will want to visit every chance they get!

Pleasing Mom, Dad, and the Teacher

When creating programs for children and youth in the library setting, it's necessary to invest time, energy, and resources into reaching out and connecting with them on their own level (as we just discussed), but it mustn't stop there. There are teams of other people invested in these young minds, and the ability to reinforce their work and support them in as many ways as possible will transform your "good" program into a great one, which will in turn speak highly to the institution itself and will bring families back for repeat visits.

The demands of modern life take a toll on families with both parents (most likely) working, school work, extracurricular activities, and day-to-day life, all vying for a chunk of everyone's time. In designing a program, be it passive or scheduled, you will never be able to please everyone by working around their schedule, but you can make an effort. By taking a simple poll of what days and time slots work best for your patrons, you can offer events at times that are convenient for the majority, rather than guessing or working with what's most convenient for yourself. You'll be doing parents and caregivers a huge favor by working with their busy schedules, and for that you'll be rewarded with return, and potentially regular, patrons.

Our spy meetings were on Tuesday afternoons by design. From working with the kids on a daily basis for six months prior to the start of the club, I surmised that Tuesday was the lightest homework day. It was also a day that most kids were able to attend as most of their extracurricular activities took place on Wednesday evenings. Thursdays were heavy homework days as we were preparing for Friday's tests, leaving Tuesday the most ideal time to meet. Though I never met with any of the teachers who were involved with my kids' lives, I was supporting them and the work they were doing by making sure the spy schedule allowed for a timely completion of projects and homework. There were a few occasions when a big school and/or community event was taking place on Tuesday evenings, so I "appealed to headquarters" and was granted permission to bump the meeting time up to allow for the agents to participate in their band concerts and neighborhood festivals.

Recently, while working at the reference desk at my current library, I received a phone call from a distressed parent. She prefaced the call by admitting that she was from a neighboring city, but wanted to know if she and her toddler were welcome at my library. "Absolutely," I said, but inquired as to why she didn't use her own city's library. It was much closer to where she lived and I knew from personal experience that it had a decent collection. It turns out that she *had* been using that library, but was made to feel uncomfortable and unwelcome after the librarians told her that she needed to keep her son's noise level down. A small piece of my heart broke at hearing this, but I was quick to assure her that we would welcome her and her son, noises and all, at our building.

When you commit to supporting parents and caregivers, then you must consent to the fact that parenting and caregiving will take place in your space. Kids will be loud, things will be broken, milk will be spilled, and you've got to be able to roll with it all. There is growth happening at all times, and when looking at situations with this mind-set, you will able to focus less on the negatives. That noisy gurgling and nonsensical babble are the first attempts at becoming verbal, and to squash that exercise slows the growth of the child, associates a negative connotation with that activity, and makes the parents/caregivers feel unwelcome and unsupported. Of course, there must be limits; we can't have kids running around screaming like wild banshees (at least not *all* the time, there is only so many ibuprofen you can take at one time after all) but allowing kids to be kids, noises, messes, and all will help to make their childhood all the richer and more colorful while adding a positive addition to the "village" that it takes to raise a child.

I have found that many adults are eager to interact with their children in a meaningful yet fun way; they just need a little motivation and guidance in getting there. Out of all the agents who were members of the Free Library of Philadelphia Espionage Agency (FLPEA), only three parents (all mothers) were engaged with the program. These parents also were made to fill out an application and fulfill one of the training requirements for membership, which the kids got a kick out of. It gave the parents a way to interact and play with their children and their children's friends. These moms became very well known throughout the course of the program as they were quick to lend a helping hand as well as encourage further exploration of topics covered. During one week, I had the agents doing binary coding, and one of the youngest agents led her caregiver and fellow agent through the process of decoding letters based on the eight-box pattern. The mother was having difficulty understanding the concept of binary code, and the young agent was able take all of the patience poured upon her (I'm sure, during all the time it took her to learn how to tie her shoes, learn her alphabet, and so on) and give it back to her mom via a lesson on coding. For what may have been the first time in her young life, the child became the teacher and the parent the student. Interactions like this allow for, and even necessitate, open and clear communication skills, patience, sequence recognition, and so forth. It's a rich learning moment for all parties involved, and now that the parent has experienced it, she can re-create similar learning scenarios on her own.

One of the most valuable skills that librarians can impart to adults in supporting them on their journey of raising children and youth is to equip them with the language and tools to create their own learning playgrounds wherever they may be. This can be done by offering training classes specifically for adults, but on a daily basis, our behavior and interactions with their children will model what it takes to assist in the growth of children's minds. What comes as second nature to many of us, thanks to the excellent training received geared toward children and youth, is a foreign school of thought to many adults. For example, during story time, having the children repeat letter sounds, words, and sentences after you will model a literacy skill to the adults in the room, and will (hopefully) encourage them to do the same. Reading techniques like changing your voice, having the child act out part of the story, or even singing the words are all viable ways to teach literacy that perhaps never crossed the mind of adults who work with finances or animals for a living. We must not take our own skill sets for granted, nor should we assume that just because someone is a parent that they know all the tips and tricks.

Many of the activities that made up the weekly missions were all done with easily accessible materials and were easy to re-create at home. By offering this type of low-tech and low-cost, yet highly engaging, educational and entertaining activity, the adults were adding things to their wheelhouse of at-home activities. This also benefits the teacher as it continues the conversation beyond the walls of the library and classroom. Learning isn't so much remembering facts and theories as much as it is training the brain to think and to solve problems. By extending conversations outside of the learning environment, children are shown that learning can take place anywhere, at any time, and with anything.

Fostering healthy relationships between children and adults is an added benefit to hosting programs where all ages are welcome. There are some children who are starved of positive adult interactions, and for them libraries can be a safe and inviting place. I had two agents in particular who were such children, and were quick to take attention (be it good or bad) from any adult within a 10-foot vicinity. Once the spy meetings started up, one of the three moms who was regularly attending with her son took these two under her wing. She praised them when they were able to make connections and solve problems on their own, and she encouraged them when they were stuck, and even helped keep them in check when their manners went out the door. This mom went above and beyond to reach out to these two girls, and it was the epitome of what a library stands for. It was a beautiful illustration of an intergenerational, interracial, interdisciplinary community hangout, and everyone was not only having a good time, but they were having fun as well.

The Power of Play

I consider it a great honor and privilege to work with children and youth, and I strive for excellence in every interaction, program, and event that I participate in. I've been fortunate to work with teams of people helping kids in settings as varied as day camps in South Africa to the Children's Museum of Houston. In all the places I've worked, never has the power of play been so evident as with the spy club at the FLP.

It's very easy to become jaded and assume the worst or least of people, especially for those of us who work with the public on a daily basis. People are rude, they take advantage of the system and entitlement runs with wild abandon. But these behaviors are all learned, and by giving children and youth the benefit of the doubt, holding them to a higher standard, and offering them programming with equally high quality can help to curb those less desirable behaviors and create better citizenry. We often live up to the expectations set upon us by outside influencers, so let's help our community and ourselves by setting the bar higher and expecting more from one another.

I couldn't tell you who was more excited about the weekly spy meetings: the kids or myself. I was giddy with anticipation as I led the agents down to their meeting room each week, for I was having the time of my life pulling off this massively involved program all on my own. Had I been a kid and my library offered a program like the spy club, I would have absolutely eaten it up. There were days when I was actually jealous of the pure and unadulterated fun the kids were having with the missions. They were playing a tailor-made, live-action, multiweek game that was not only fun, but was teaching them concepts that they will take with them for years to come.

By incorporating various forms of play (free, structured, group, individual, etc.), the kids were able to interact with one another and the content, in new and exciting ways each week. Membership to the FLPEA gave the kids a confidence boost that had them literally standing taller and speaking with gusto. New vocabulary words were dropped into daily conversation, and confidence to speak up to help solve a problem, on homework or in life, was a common occurrence.

Many of these agents weren't afforded the luxury of summer camps or paid after-school programs. They were at the library because it was free and that's what their families could afford. In school many of them faced hurdles as they were quickly left behind, with little to no hope of catching up. Whether they didn't test well or they didn't apply themselves was a moot point as there was always a backstory to each of their test scores. Some truly were trying hard, and just falling short. Others weren't putting forth any effort because they had failed so much that they came to expect little else of themselves. Still others came from rough home situations and were too preoccupied with those issues to focus on school. As with everything else in life, there were myriad stories dictating each child's life. The unfortunate thing is that the tools we have to measure intelligence (at this age, school tests) don't take any of the aforementioned into account. They're simply a measurement device for rote memorization, which is unfair and terribly inaccurate for measuring intelligence.

One second-grade girl in particular, we'll call her B, was a particularly difficult child to work with when it came time for homework. She would distract herself and the other students, and would even try to distract me with anything and everything under the sun before she even laid eyes on her homework—that is, if she brought it with her. She was very outgoing and could talk with anyone about anything. Admittedly, I am no doctor, but what I was seeing with B didn't seem to be a medical issue; rather it seemed to be an issue of deep self-doubt and low self-esteem despite her bubbly and social persona. She consistently scored low on school exams and was only concerned with those red Fs because of the wrath she would face from her father. She cared very little for her teacher and the repeated comments of low expectations that her teacher made about her in front of the class. Everyone knew that B wasn't smart, and would always come in last on all the tests. This broke my heart, and try as I might, no matter what kind of game I turned her homework into, she refused to apply herself. This is why I was so shocked to see B take the lead on missions and actively solve problems with a clear and concise thought process.

Over the course of the semester that spy club was in session, B proved to be one of the most able and adept agents on the case. She was brilliant! All she needed was a fresh slate, an environment that accepted failure as part of the solution process, and some play infused within it to prove to us all, but, most importantly, to herself, that she was a valuable and intelligent person. She had some of the most unique solutions to problems, and fully embraced the positive aspects of failure. B's case is not an anomaly, for several of the students had no idea how much they were capable of. They thought I was crazy to entrust the entire mission to them at the beginning of the club, but I believed in them from the get-go. It was themselves that they had to prove their worth to, and week after week, as they completed more and more complex missions, they realized that they did indeed have what it takes to be a part of the most elite espionage agency in the library world.

The agents eventually tracked down the missing cryptex and the rogue librarian who stole it. When it was returned to the agents, they completed the five-letter code to open the lock and reveal a secret "written by" Benjamin Franklin himself. It was his darkest and deepest secret that he had written on a scroll, locked in a cryptex, and hidden within the FLP. It read:

I never passed the second grade.

This is true, one of our founding fathers, though he was undeniably brilliant, didn't do well in formal education, and as an elementary aged child, his home life didn't allow for the time commitment that was the school day. I chose this as his secret, for it was a message that would ring true with many of the agents. It showed them that despite his setbacks, Benjamin Franklin went on to do great things, and so too can they.

It was through the power of play that this group of kids learned how to read maps, crack codes, solve problems, and create tangible solutions (to name just a few things). On every level, play is a powerful tool for discovery. It helps kids to make sense out of things, by encouraging exploration of the unknown. It builds up social skills (as in the spy club's case) as the missions were often group activities that had to be worked out together. Communication skills, mediation, and teamwork were all required to get the job done. The agents were players in a live-action game that fully engulfed them. By joining the FLPEA, they were a part of something much bigger than themselves, which gave them a sense of purpose and of pride that they carried with them. Most of all, they were having fun. In undergrad, I was taught to get kids to have so much fun that they don't realize that anything educational is happening. This is what I strive for every time I create a program. I want it to be so heavily focused on an aspect of playing that the fun factor unconsciously becomes associated with learning and mind growth.

Allowing yourself to become fully absorbed in the program at hand will facilitate a learning environment that is fun and exciting. Ultimately, it is the fun factor that will bring patrons back to you for repeat visits. If you cannot enjoy the program yourself, then how in the world can you expect your participants to enjoy it? Go ahead, and allow yourself to get a little batty. After all, we do work in the most magical place of all!

> ### The BIG Picture
>
> By placing yourself into your kids' shoes, you can begin to anticipate their actions and curate an environment, collection, and programs that will cater to and engage them. Let yourself revel in the joy and excitement that your patrons bring, but know where to draw the line and which rules you need in place to ensure a safe and productive environment. By harnessing the power of play, you can transform your library into an exciting and innovative learning playground!

Reflection Questions

1. How can you transform the rules you have in place to reflect positive language? (No running = Walk like a penguin)
2. How can you incorporate caregivers and adults into your programs?
3. How will you harness the power of play?

APPENDIX

Participants

In the table below, fill in as much information as possible. This process is intended to help clearly define your audience. For some of the sections, interview questions may be in order with both the students and the teachers. Your objective for this chart is to fill in as much information as you can gather in regard to what is popular with your intended audience. It is not necessary to fill out all rows; however, the more information you have about your intended user group, the better prepared and targeted your program will be.

Age range	
Books	
Games	
Movies	
TV shows	
School topics	

Goals

Now that your user group is clearly defined and you've gathered some information about what they're interested in, it's time to start outlining the goals for the program. Use this space to work out WHY this program should be offered. Clear and concise language will help direct you in a clear and concise direction.

What is the main goal for the participants?

Main goal	

What is the main goal for you?

Main goal	

What is the main goal for the library?

Main goal	

Program

When determining what type of program you want to offer, several factors must be taken into consideration.

What is your time frame for creating this program?	
What is your time frame for implementation?	
What is your budget to work with?	
How many staff members are needed?	
How many volunteers are needed?	
Will this event require registration?	
Will this program have a participant limit?	
What space will your program be presented in?	
Will you partner with any outside organization for this program?	

How to Use This Program Template

Program guide:
This page will serve as your overview for the program. Keep it with you, or nearby, during the implementation so that you can quickly refer to your intended goals and schedule.

Materials needed:
In this table, write out each and every item that you need to collect for the program. Once you've acquired an item, check it off the list. The sooner you are able to create this list, the more organized your planning will be.

Preparation:
Write out all of the things you need to do in order to prepare for your program. *Gather materials. Cut out shapes. Contact educators. And so on.* If you write out the to-dos in chronological order, then by glancing at this sheet you'll be able to tell exactly how prepared (or unprepared) you are for the program.

In-depth lesson information:
If you are the type to create skeletal or bullet-point talking points, then move on to the next page. For those that want to write out very detailed information paragraphs for the program at hand, use this space to do so.

Resource list:
Use this page to keep a running tab of what resources you use for your program planning and implementation. Regardless of whether or not you hand out a resource bibliography at the end of each event, it's always good to know exactly what sources you consulted.

Quantification and assessment:
After the dust has settled and wild rumpus comes to an end, use this sheet to make a record of how many attended your program as well as the skills that were utilized/built upon. Be as detailed as you can, for when it comes time to pitch another program, these data, paired with anecdotal observations, will give your pitch a solid backing.

Program Guide

Program Title: _____

Goals

_____
_____
_____
_____

Program Description

Program lead: _____
Room: _____
Setup: _____
Age range: _____

Program schedule:

Time	Activity

Materials Needed	X

Preparation

Description	X

In-Depth Lesson Information

Resource List	X

Quantification and Assessment

Total Participants: _____

Concept	Description
Science	
Technology	
Engineering	
Art	
Math	
Print motivation	
Narrative skills	
Vocabulary	
Phonological awareness	
Literacy	
Initiative	
Diversity	
Creativity	
Teamwork and collaboration	
Critical thinking	
Adaptability	

Index

Active listening, 26
American Disability Act, 34
American Library Association, 62
American Library Services to Children's Dia programs, 33
Audience: active listening and, 26; age appropriate, and language, 57; and story hook, 43–45

Base, Graeme, 38
The Birdcage, 15
Bizzle, Ben, 83
Body language, 26–27
Book collection: categorizing, 93; digital databases, 93; in libraries, 92
Books, 20
Branding: clubs, 81; logos, 81. *See also* Marketing; Promotion
Bullet-formatted program, 57–58
Bullet-style goals, 41
Bullock, Sandra, 32
Bullying, 16

Catalog search engines, 93
Center for Children's Books at the University of Wisconsin–Madison, 33–34
Chicago Cub, 80
Children: active listening and, 26; belonging to LGBTQI+ community, 34; body language and, 26–27; communication skills with, 26; organized chaos and, 28–31; trust, gaining, 32–35
Classroom learning: and communication with educators, 89; and experimentations, 88; and libraries, 87; math curriculum, 85–86
Club-based programs, 53; marketing, 79–89; and parents, 94–97; and sense of ownership, 83–85; and teachers, 94–97
Communication: age appropriate audience and, 57; developing skills, with children, 26; with educators, 89. *See also* Language
Computers: accessibility and libraries, 21; and learning environment, 22
Cultural competence, 32
Culture: libraries and, 17–20; local art and clubs, 19; teaching about, 33

Dictionary.com, 4
Digital databases, 93
DIY (do-it-yourself) trend, 74

Einstein, Albert, 9
The Eleventh Hour (Base), 38
Environmental Protection Agency (EPA), 3
Escape from Mr. Lemoncello's Library (Grabenstein), 38
External motivation, 38

Franklin, Benjamin, 19
Free Library Foundation, xii
Free Library of Philadelphia (FLP), xii, 6, 81
Free Library of Philadelphia Espionage Agency (FLPEA), xiii–xiv, 8, 54
Free play, 5–9

Game design, 38; external motivation, 38; intrinsic motivation, 38
Game mechanics, 9
Gamification, 3
Goals: bullet-style, 41; of participants, 42; of story programming, 41–42
Grabenstein, Chris, 38
Group story, 6

Habitica, 3
#WeNeedDiverseBooks, 33
Homeless people, 34–35
Hook, stories, 43–45

In-depth program planning, 56–57; benefits, 56; information translation for age-appropriate audience, 57
Inquiry-based learning, 84
Inquiry-based programs, 57, 66
Interdisciplinary curriculum, 65
Internet, 21
Intrinsic motivation, 38

Language: and age appropriate audience, 57; and creativity, 93–94. *See also* Communication
Librarians: children's, 92; communicating about emotions with children, 27; knowledge, 69; marketing programs, 82; role in creating book collections, 20; teaching techniques, 47

Library/ies: book collection, 92; children's, 92; and classroom curriculum, 87; computer accessibility and, 21; culture and, 17–20; diversity of text in, 20–22; shelf placement in, 93; staff, 22; welcoming space, 92
Literacy Enrichment After-School Program (LEAP), xi
Literacy skills, 69
Logos, 81

Magnus Effect, 68
Maker movement, 72–77
Maker spaces, 74–75
Marketing: branding, 81; campaigns, 82; club programs, 79–89; logos, 81; testimonials, 81; traditional media, 81. *See also* Promotion
Math curriculum, 85–86
Mobile apps, 3
Motivation: external, 38; intrinsic, 38

Narrative skills, 70
National Center for Education Statistics, xi

Organized chaos, 28–31
Oxford Living Dictionary, 4

Parents: and club-based programs, 94–97; gaining trust of, 32–35
Passive programs, 40
Pennsylvania System of School Assessment (PSSA) scores, xi
pH testing experiment, 88
Pinterest, 62
Play: benefits of learning through, 9–12; defined, 4; described, 1–5; free *vs.* structured, 5–9; power of, 97–99
Pop culture, 38
Posters, 82
Program planning, 51–63; in-depth, 56–57; introduction, 56; skeletal, 57–59; supporting activities and, 60–62; time frame for, 53; writing weekly/daily lesson plans, 55–56. *See also* Club-based programs

Promotion: of club programs, 79–89; posters, 82; testimonials, 81

Quipu (kee-poo), 86

Role-play, 16

Safe space, 13–14
Sense of ownership, and club programs, 83–85
Setting the scene, 45–48
Skeletal program planning, 57–59
Start a Revolution: Stop Acting Like a Library (Bizzle), 83
STEAM (science, technology, engineering, art, and math), 73–77
STEM (science, technology, engineering, and math), 2; incorporating into public programs, 68; and marketing club programs, 83; specific roles, 68
Story programming, 37–48; game design, 38; goals of, 41–42; hook, 43–45; passive programs, 40; planning, 51–63; pop culture, 38; setting the scene, 45–48. *See also* Program planning
Strategic Initiatives (SI), xii
Structured play, 5–9

Take-apart club, 61
Teachers: and club-based programs, 94–97; role of, 47, 87; use of game strategies, 3
Testimonials, 81
Toyota Prius, 3
Traditional media, 81
Trust: gaining children, 32–35; gaining parents, 32–35; multlingual interaction and, 34
Trust test, 32
28 Days, 32

United Nations' Convention on the Rights of the Child, 2

Whistle-blowing, 80
World Wide Web, 21
Writing weekly/daily lesson plans, 55–56

About the Author

BRITTANY R. JACOBS is an author and illustrator of children's picture books, a children's services associate at Naperville Public Library, and an educational programming consultant. She is currently pursuing her MS in library and information science with the School of Information Sciences at the University of Illinois Champaign/Urbana. Jacobs is a PAL (Published and Listed) member of the Society of Children's Book Writers and Illustrators, as well as a member of the American Library Association and Association for Library Service to Children. From working with community centers in South Africa to her work at the Free Library of Philadelphia, creating innovative ways for children and youth to explore the world around them has always been a passion of Jacobs.

Made in the USA
Columbia, SC
06 February 2025